THE VOICE
THAT CHALLENGED
A NATION

THE VOICE THAT CHALLENGED A NATION

Marian Anderson

AND THE STRUGGLE FOR EQUAL RIGHTS

by Russell Freedman

SCHOLASTIC INC.

New York Toronto London Auckland Sydney
Mexico City New Delhi Hong Kong Buenos Aires

ISBN 0-439-79934-1

12 11 10 9 8 7 6 5 4 3 2   5 6 7 8 9 10/0

Printed in the U.S.A.

First Scholastic printing, September 2005

The text was set in 11.5-point Sabon.

Book design by Sylvia Frezzolini Severance

To Emmanuel d'Amonville

"A friendship as had master'd time"

Contents

One   Easter Sunday, April 9, 1939   1

Two   Twenty-five Cents a Song   5

Three   A Voice in a Thousand   21

Four   Marian Fever   33

Five   Banned by the DAR   47

Six   Singing to the Nation   59

Seven   Breaking Barriers   71

Eight   "What I Had Was Singing"   91

Chapter Notes   95

Selected Bibliography   101

Selected Discography   105

Acknowledgments and Picture Credits   107

Index   109

THE VOICE
THAT CHALLENGED
A NATION

Standing on the steps of the Lincoln Memorial,
Marian Anderson sings to a crowd of 75,000 people.

One

EASTER SUNDAY, APRIL 9, 1939

Lord I got a right,

Lord I got a right,

Lord I got a right,

I got a right to the tree of life.

African American Spiritual

Despite cold and threatening weather, the crowd began to assemble long before the concert was to begin. People arrived singly and in pairs and in large animated groups. Soon the streets leading to the Mall in Washington, D.C., were jammed with thousands of people heading for the Lincoln Memorial.

The earliest arrivals found places as close as possible to the steps of the great marble monument. As the crowd grew, it spread back along the Mall, stretching around both sides of the long reflecting pool and extending beyond to the base of the Washington Monument, three-quarters of a mile away. Baby carriages were parked among the trees. Folks cradled sleeping infants in their arms and held youngsters by the hand or propped up on their shoulders. Uniformed Boy Scouts moved through the festive holiday throng handing out programs.

Anticipating a huge turnout, the National Park Service had enlisted the help of some five hundred Washington police officers. By five o'clock that afternoon, when the concert was scheduled to start, an estimated 75,000 people had gathered on the Mall. They waited patiently under overcast skies, bundled up against the brisk wind that whipped in from the Potomac River. They had come on this chilly Easter Sunday to hear one of the great voices of the time and to demonstrate their support for racial justice in the nation's capital.

Singing to the nation from the steps of the Lincoln Memorial.

Marian Anderson had been applauded by many of the crowned heads of Europe. She had been welcomed at the White House, where she sang for the president and first lady, Franklin and Eleanor Roosevelt. She had performed before appreciative audiences in concert halls across the United States. But because she was an African American, she had been denied the right to sing at Constitution Hall, Washington's largest and finest auditorium. The Daughters of the American Revolution, the patriotic organization that owned Constitution Hall, had ruled several years earlier that black artists would not be permitted to appear there.

News of the DAR's ban had caused an angry controversy and set the stage for a historic event in the struggle for civil rights. Working behind the scenes, a group of influential political figures had found an appropriate concert space for Anderson. Barred from Constitution Hall, she would give a free open-air concert on the steps of the Lincoln Memorial.

Shortly before the concert got under way, the skies above Washington began to clear. Clouds, which had shadowed the monument, skittered away to the north, and the late-afternoon sun broke through to bathe the reflecting pool and shine on the gaily dressed Easter crowd. Secretary of the Interior Harold L. Ickes appeared on the speaker's platform. He introduced Miss Anderson, and she stepped forward to the bank of microphones.

The massive figure of Abraham Lincoln gazed down at her as she looked out at the expectant throng. Silencing the ovation with a slight wave of her hand, she paused. A profound hush settled over the crowd. For that moment, Marian Anderson seemed vulnerable and alone. Then she closed her eyes, lifted her head, clasped her hands before her, and began to sing.

Marian Anderson in 1898, one year old.

Two

TWENTY-FIVE CENTS A SONG

"I sang naturally, as free as a bird."

Marian Anderson loved to sing, and she loved to listen while others were singing. At Philadelphia's Stanton Elementary School, her fourth-grade classroom was next to the room where the children went to learn songs. On those days, she remembered, "I did not hear a word my teacher spoke. I was as completely in that other room as one could be while one's body was elsewhere. When the day came for our class to go there for singing, I was the happiest child in the school."

She sang for the sheer joy of singing, and her uniquely beautiful voice delighted everyone who knew her. At the Union Baptist Church, where her family worshiped, she had been an enthusiastic member of the junior choir ever since her sixth birthday. Alexander Robinson, the man who led the choir, recognized the youngster's musical gifts and her eagerness to learn and to perform. And he discovered that she had an unusually wide vocal range. She could sing any part with ease. While her voice had the rich, dark timbre of contralto, the lowest female voice, she had no trouble with the ringing tones of soprano, the highest. Soon she was singing well enough to be entrusted with solos when the junior choir performed at the church's main Sunday service.

Marian's aunt Mary sang in the senior choir. She began to take her niece to local benefits and community events, where Marian would be asked to sing a song or two and would earn twenty-five or even fifty cents. As word of her talent spread, Aunt Mary had handbills printed with a picture of Marian and the words "Come and hear the baby contralto, ten years old."

About this time, Marian was invited to join the People's Chorus, made up of a hundred voices recruited from black church choirs all over the city. She became one of the youngest and smallest members of the Chorus. The director, Emma Azalia Hackley, wanted to make sure that Marian would not be lost in the crowd, so she had her stand on a chair whenever she sang a solo. "I want her to feel elevated," said Hackley, "and I want no one in the back of the hall to have the slightest difficulty in seeing her."

Marian lived with her parents, John and Anna Anderson, and two younger sisters, Alyse and Ethel May, in South Philadelphia, where she was born on February 27, 1897, three decades after the end of slavery in America. She grew up in a poor but vibrant neighborhood, home to Irish, Italian, and Jewish immigrants and to African American families that had come up from the rural South to seek job opportunities in the city. "I don't remember being conscious of any difference between me and white children when I was a small child," Anderson told an interviewer years later. "I think this was because there were white and Negro families mingled on our block and all the children played together. We were in and out of each other's houses all day long."

Blacks—the polite term at that time was Negro—and whites lived side by side in South Philadelphia, but as Marian grew older, she learned that prejudice and discrimination often kept the races apart. Blacks worshiped in segregated churches, which provided sanctuary against the pain of discrimination. At Union Baptist Church, Marian heard a gospel of dignity and pride.

"There were times when we heard our relatives and friends talking," she remembered, "and we knew we might come in contact with [racial discrimination]. In some stores we might have to stand around longer than other people until we were waited on. There were times when we stood on a street corner, waiting for a trolley car, and the motorman would pass us by. There were places in town where all people could go, and there were others where some of us could not go. There were girls we played with, and others we didn't. There were parties we went to, and some we didn't. We were interested in neither the places nor the people who did not want us."

Marian's grammar school, like her neighborhood, was racially mixed, with

Anna Anderson (rear) *with her three daughters* (front row, from left), *Alyse, Marian, and Ethel May.*

black students and white students, but all the teachers were white. In Philadelphia at the time, black teachers were allowed to teach only in schools attended primarily by black students.

John Anderson supported his family by selling coal and ice at the Reading Terminal Market in downtown Philadelphia. On Sundays he served as chief usher at the Union Baptist Church. "He was tall and very fine looking," Marian recalled, "and oh, how happy he was on holidays to take us out. He'd plan a picnic and I remember him so clearly getting things together for our outings." One day he bought the family a piano from his brother Harold, who had it in his home where

*John Berkley
Anderson,
Marian's father.*

no one used it. Though there was no money for lessons, Marian and her sisters taught themselves to play some simple melodies. They would sit on their father's knee as he sat at the piano, guiding his hands as they tried to teach him what they had learned on their own.

In 1909 John Anderson was accidentally struck on the head while working at the market. He never recovered from his injuries, and shortly after Christmas that year he died of heart failure at the age of thirty-four, leaving Marian's mother to raise their three girls. Marian was twelve years old. "My sisters and I did not put it into so many words," she recalled, "but we knew that tragedy had moved into our home, and we knew, too, that our lives would change."

Marian, her mother, and her sisters were taken in by her father's parents, whose small house was also home to an aunt and uncle, two cousins, and, at times, one or two boarders who contributed to the rent and expenses. Marian remembered her grandmother Isabella as an imposing woman, tall and imperious, who ruled her family with an iron hand. "She liked to remind people that she was part [American] Indian," Marian recalled. Isabella towered over her soft-spoken

Isabella Anderson (seated), Marian's grandmother, and Mary Anderson, Marian's aunt.

husband, Benjamin, a deeply religious man who had converted to the Jewish faith. Marian's grandfather referred to himself as a Black Jew and practiced his adopted religion in a crowded household of devout Baptists. He kept the Sabbath on Saturday, observed Passover and other important Jewish holidays, and belonged to a small neighborhood congregation, whose members called themselves Hebrews or Israelites.

Marian's grandfather, Benjamin Anderson, was a convert to Judaism. He belonged to a congregation similar to the one shown here, photographed in Harlem in 1929.

Marian's widowed mother was determined to keep her family together. Years earlier, before her marriage, Anna had taught school in Lynchburg, Virginia, but she lacked the credentials needed to teach in Philadelphia. To support her daughters, she took in laundry and later found a job as a cleaning woman at Wanamaker's Department Store downtown. Marian and her sisters helped out by delivering bundles of laundry their mother had done, by running errands, and by scrubbing the white marble steps in front of the neat row houses that lined so many South Philadelphia streets. "So I scrubbed steps," Marian recalled, "and I would get five or ten cents, or whatever. I did steps for four or five different people."

Marian completed eight grades at Stanton Elementary School. When she graduated, the family felt that they could not afford to send her on to high school. Expenses for books, clothes, and social events would be more than they could handle, and in any case they needed the money that Marian could earn by doing domestic work for neighbors and by singing.

By now she was a member of the senior choir at Union Baptist Church, which gave her the chance to learn more difficult and varied music. She continued to sing with the junior choir as well, with the hundred-voice People's Chorus, and at local church and social events. She had learned to accompany herself on the piano, and the more she performed, the more calls there were for her to sing in other places. The twenty-five or fifty cents she had earned as a small girl rose to one or two dollars or more. "Soon I was emboldened to establish a minimum of five dollars for an appearance," she recalled. "What did I do with the fee? I gave each of my sisters a dollar, two to Mother, and one I kept. In those days, I was not dressed so grandly that I needed taxis to deliver me to the places where I sang. A trolley car sufficed, and the fare was my only expenditure."

Marian never missed a Sunday at Union Baptist Church with either the junior or senior choir. The congregation wanted to show its appreciation, so one Sunday morning the pastor, the Reverend Wesley Parks, took up a special collection for her after the regular collection. The proceeds, $17.02, were turned over to Mrs. Anderson to be used for anything Marian needed. What she needed most was an evening dress to wear at her singing appearances. Marian and her mother went shopping, but when they saw how much department-store dresses cost, they used the collection money to buy some white satin material and make a dress themselves, using Mrs. Anderson's sewing machine. "This was my evening dress for quite some time," Marian recalled, "and in some ways it made me happier than the one that would have cost fourteen ninety-eight."

She had many opportunities to sing in public, and as she gained confidence, she began to dream of a career as a singer. So far she had never had a chance to benefit from formal voice training. One of her admirers was Roland Hayes, a young black tenor who appeared often at the Union Baptist Church. The son of a former slave, Hayes was recognized as one of the finest singers in America. In his church recitals he broke with tradition and featured classical songs by European composers along with traditional African American spirituals. Even so, he faced the same barriers of racial prejudice that confronted all African American artists of the time. Since black performers were not welcome at most of the country's concert halls, he sang mainly at black churches and colleges. Later he went to Europe, hoping to earn the success that was denied him at home. There he became the first African American to achieve an international reputation as a concert singer.

When Hayes first heard Marian sing, he urged her to start professional studies, but her family had no money for high school, let alone voice lessons. Once again the congregation of Union Baptist Church stepped in to help. When they learned that Marian wanted to attend a certain music school, the church members promised to guarantee her tuition.

"I knew the music school I wanted to go to," she later said. "It doesn't exist anymore, but at the time it had a fine reputation and as far as I was concerned represented everything a singer could wish for."

She went to the school to enroll and took her place in line with the other prospective students. When her turn came, the young woman who was handing out application forms didn't seem to notice her: "She looked over my head when it got to be my turn, and took care of one after another of the ones behind me until I was the only one left. She spoke to me then, but in a different tone of voice from the one she'd used to the other people. 'What do you want?' was what she said."

Marian asked for an application form. The young woman looked at her coldly and replied, "We don't take colored."

Marian never forgot the stinging sense of rejection that came with hearing those words. "It was a tremendously great shock," she recalled, "and I was very unprepared. . . . I promise you, I was as sick as if she'd hit me with her fist right in the middle of my stomach, and I mean really, physically sick. I wonder I didn't

Tenor Roland Hayes, an early admirer of Marian Anderson and an influential role model. He was the first African American classical singer to win an international reputation.

throw up right there. . . . I don't know how I got out of the place and home. All I could think of was how could anybody who was as pretty as that, and had a chance to listen to music all day long, act that way and say such a terrible thing. And then I'd think, 'Can't I sing, can't I be a singer because I'm colored?'"

At the time, most of Philadelphia's music conservatories accepted white students only. And only rarely was a black music student accepted for individual study by a white teacher. Marian found her first voice teacher in her own neighborhood. Mary Saunders Patterson was a well-known black soprano who lived just a few blocks away. Marian met her through a family friend who had offered to pay for her lessons, but Patterson refused to take the friend's money. She believed that young people just starting out in their careers should not feel burdened by obligations, no matter how unselfish the offer of help might be. Patterson normally charged a dollar a lesson, but she offered to give Marian lessons free of charge.

Until then, Marian had never really thought much about vocal technique. "I sang naturally, as free as a bird," she said. Studying with Patterson, she began to understand that the voice could be controlled and channeled. Patterson taught her how to project and focus her voice, how to aim it toward a corner of the ceiling, high up where the walls joined, and make it heard at the very back of a theater without straining it.

Patterson also introduced Marian to a whole new repertory of songs. She had grown up singing the old slave songs called spirituals, the hymns she had learned in church, and songs by popular American composers, such as Stephen Foster. But if she wanted to become a concert artist, she would be expected to perform a variety of songs in their native tongue, including arias from Italian operas, French melodies, and German ballads, or lieder—poems set to music. These were the songs by European classical composers like Giuseppe Verdi and Franz Schubert that she had heard Roland Hayes sing in church, and that she now began to learn.

After several months, Patterson felt that Marian was advanced enough to move on to another teacher. Once again Philadelphia's black community came to her aid. In June 1915 the People's Chorus gave a benefit concert to support Marian's further studies, raising about $250. Part of the money was set aside for lessons with Agnes Reifsnyder, one of the few white voice teachers in Philadelphia willing to accept black students. Like Marian, Reifsnyder was a contralto, so she was well equipped to teach the kinds of songs especially suitable for Marian's voice. The rest of the money raised by the benefit concert made it possible for Marian to begin high school at long last. In the fall of 1915, several months before her nineteenth birthday, she entered William Penn High School, and each year after that the black community raised additional funds so that her schooling would not be interrupted.

While she dreamed of a singing career, she knew she would have to support herself and help her family when she finished school, so she took the high school's secretarial course, studying bookkeeping, shorthand, and typing. But her heart wasn't in those studies, and after three unhappy years she was able to transfer to the newly established South Philadelphia High School for Girls, where she enrolled

Marian (center) *with unidentified friends around 1915, when she started high school.*

in an academic course, emphasizing music. Several years older than any of the other girls, she was one of the school's few black students. Her classmates would remember her as a shy and often self-conscious young woman who kept to herself and concentrated on her musical studies. She was "interested in pretty much nothing else but singing," one student recalled, "not taking part in dances or things like that."

During her high school years, Marian continued to sing at church and social events and, increasingly, at concerts out of town. In 1917, just before Christmas, she was invited to take part in a gala concert at the Georgia State Industrial College, a black college in Savannah. She had never visited the Deep South before, and on this trip, for the first time, she experienced the strict "Jim Crow" laws that enforced racial segregation throughout the South.

By 1918 Marian was singing regularly at church, school, and social events.
This photo was taken when she appeared as a soloist for the CLEF Club at the
Philadelphia Academy of Music.

She traveled with her mother from Philadelphia to Washington, D.C., where they had to change trains to continue south. At Washington's Union Station black and white passengers were separated. The Andersons' bags were taken to the first coach on the train headed south—the Jim Crow coach reserved for blacks. As Marian recalled, the car was dirty inside and out, the windows were badly in need of washing, and the ventilation and lighting were poor. When the air became stuffy and the windows were raised, smoke and soot from the engine directly ahead poured into the car. "I had heard about Jim Crow," Marian wrote later, "but meeting it bit deeply into the soul. . . . I had looked closely at my people in that train. Some seemed to be embarrassed to the core. Others appeared to accept the situation as if it were beyond repair."

In the segregated South, Jim Crow laws required black train passengers to use separate coaches and waiting rooms.

Arriving in Savannah after an overnight trip, Marian and her mother were greeted warmly by school officials and were put up at the home of the college president. That evening an audience of nearly a thousand people turned out for the concert in Savannah's new Municipal Auditorium, whites sitting in the boxes and dress circle, blacks in segregated orchestra or gallery seats. "[Marian] Anderson, the soloist, has one of the most remarkable voices ever heard in Savannah," reported the *Savannah Morning News*.

By now she was receiving so many invitations that she had trouble keeping up with her high school studies. Roland Hayes invited her to sing on some of his own programs. She traveled to Tennessee, where she gave a week of concerts at black churches and colleges. And she won a scholarship to take a six-week summer course at the Chicago Conservatory of Music.

In Wilmington, Delaware, at a reception following a concert, she was introduced to a tall young man named Orpheus Fisher, who, like her, was still in high school. He fell for the shy singer with the soft laughter and huge sparkling eyes who was almost as tall as he, and Marian, as she later admitted, was attracted to Orpheus. They saw a good deal of each other. It wasn't long before Orpheus suggested that they run away and get married. But Marian, determined to build a career, wasn't interested in discussing marriage. "I was busy with the beginnings of my concert life," she said later, "and I thought there was no great hurry." Orpheus persisted, and in the years that followed he kept in touch with Marian as she traveled around the world. He never gave up hope that one day he would persuade her to marry him.

Meanwhile, the principal of Marian's high school, Dr. Lucy Langdon Wilson, had been following the young singer's progress with great interest. Convinced that Marian had a great future ahead of her, Wilson helped arrange an audition with Giuseppe Boghetti, a well-known voice coach who had studios in both Philadelphia and New York. Boghetti was short, stocky, and dynamic, a demanding teacher with a vast store of knowledge about vocal technique and a stern manner with his students. More than once students had been seen leaving his studio in tears. He insisted at first that he was much too busy to see Marian. He wanted no new students, he said. But finally, as a favor, he agreed to hear her sing one song.

Marian was so nervous when she arrived at Boghetti's studio that she sang her single song, "Deep River," without once looking at him. When she finished,

Boghetti seemed stunned. Finally, he turned to her. "I will make room for you right away," he said, "and I will need only two years with you. After that, you will be able to go anywhere and sing for anybody."

Again there was no money for lessons. Most of Marian's earnings from concert appearances went to her mother, who was still taking in laundry and scrubbing floors, and to her sisters, who were still in school. And again the congregation at Union Baptist Church came to Marian's aid, organizing a benefit concert that raised $566 so that she could study with Boghetti. Despite his prediction, he would remain her voice teacher for many years to come.

On June 20, 1921, soon after she began her lessons, Marian graduated from the South Philadelphia High School for Girls. She was twenty-four years old.

The 1921 graduating class of the South Philadelphia High School for Girls. Marian Anderson is in the second row from the back, second from left.

Renaissance Hall
138th Street and 7th Avenue

Monday Evening
February 18th 1924
At 8:15 o'clock

Song Recital

By
MARIAN ANDERSON
Contralto

William Leonard King
Accompanist

PROGRAM

I.
a. Caro mio ben..Giuseppe Giordani
b. Gia il sole dal Gange..Alessandro Scarlatti
c. La colomba..Kurt Schindler

II.
a. O Thou Billowy Harvest Field...........................Sergei Rachmaninoff
b. Songs My Mother Taught Me...............................Anton Dvorák
c. Zion Hallelujah, A Negro Spiritual.....................R. Nathaniel Dett

III.
a. Morgen..Richard Strauss
b. Haidenröslein..Franz Schubert
c. Aufenthalt..Franz Schubert

IV.

During the early 1920s, Marian Anderson
appeared regularly with her accompanist, Billy King.

Three

A VOICE IN A THOUSAND

"Does 44A have another song?"

After finishing high school, Marian was free to tour more widely than before. She teamed up with an energetic young accompanist, a pianist named William "Billy" King. They had fliers printed and sent them out to dozens of black colleges and churches. One appearance led to another, and soon they began to appear at theaters and small concert halls as well. "These theater appearances gave me a personal sense of accomplishment," Marian recalled. "Theaters were places where people with well-known names gave their performances. I began to feel that this was turning into a career."

Like most people during the 1920s, Marian and Billy traveled mainly by train. In the South the races were strictly segregated by law, not just on railroads but on streetcars and buses, in schools, restaurants, hotels, theaters, and parks, and even in cemeteries and at drinking fountains. Train passengers had to use separate waiting rooms, marked by signs saying FOR WHITES and FOR COL-ORED. Riding in the shabby Jim Crow car became part of Marian and Billy's travel routine. Since hotels did not accept blacks, Marian usually stayed in guesthouses at the black colleges they visited, while Billy bunked in the men's dormitory or at the black YMCA. When they appeared at black churches, they were put up at private homes.

"On a daily basis, taking a train, getting a car, getting a meal, getting a hotel

In the South, strict segregation laws kept races apart in theaters, on public transportation, and in other areas of everyday life.

William L. King, the young pianist, organist, and choir master who was Marian Anderson's regular accompanist.

room, getting your laundry done, finding a place to practice—everyone takes these things for granted when one travels today," violinist Isaac Stern observed many years later. But back then, when Marian Anderson and Billy King were touring segregated America, "you could take nothing for granted except that you would be shunted to a third- or fourth-class accommodation and some of your personal needs would not be taken care of very quickly."

Marian and Billy earned $100 for an appearance, which they split between them. Out of that they had to pay their own traveling expenses. Even so, Marian was able to save enough to help her mother make a down payment on a small house in South Philadelphia, across the street from her grandmother's place. For the first time since John Anderson's death, Marian, her mother, and her sisters had a home of their own. Ethel May and Alyse shared one of the bedrooms, while Marian and her mother slept in the other. The little house also had an extra bathroom, and Marian had it converted into a rehearsal studio where she could practice without disturbing the entire household.

Her reputation was growing. In 1923 she became the first black concert artist to record Negro spirituals for a major American recording company, the Victor Talking Machine Company. She also became the first black vocalist to appear as a soloist with the Philharmonic Society at Philadelphia's prestigious Academy of Music. "It is too much to say that Miss Anderson is as yet a great artist," wrote one critic. "But it is not too much to say that she has one of the most superb contralto voices that has been heard in Philadelphia for a very long time."

Meanwhile, she continued her voice lessons in Philadelphia with Giuseppe Boghetti. It was in his studio that she became aware of the meaning of professionalism for a public performer: "I learned that the purpose of all the exercises

Giuseppe Boghetti, Marian's demanding voice coach.

and labors was to give you a thoroughly reliable foundation and to make sure you could do your job under any circumstances. There is no shortcut. You must understand the how and why of what you are doing. If you do, you can give an acceptable performance even when you are indisposed."

In 1924 Anderson was offered the chance to give a recital at New York City's Town Hall, where young artists often were presented to the city's audiences for the first time. Boghetti had been working with her on expanding her repertoire of art songs, and now he encouraged her to prepare an ambitious program of works by Italian, German, and English composers. She rehearsed for months. But when she stepped onto the Town Hall stage the evening of the recital, her heart sank. Boghetti had promised a full house, but in fact, as Marian could see, the hall was no more than a third full.

The next morning the newspaper reviews were not complimentary. While the critics praised Marian's voice, they found fault with her singing technique and suggested that she still had a lot to learn. "[Miss Anderson] should devote more time to earnest, consistent study and less to the concert stage," said one critic.

Devastated by the harsh notices, Marian vowed never to sing again. "I was embarrassed that I had tried to sing in one of New York's concert halls without being fully ready," she admitted later, "and I went back to Philadelphia deeply disturbed. I did not want to see any music; I did not want to hear any; I did not want to make a career of it. . . . The dream was over."

Boghetti saw how deeply shaken she was, and he did not press her. For months she refused to sing in public. But gradually her depression lifted, and as she kept rehashing the Town Hall recital in her mind, she came to realize that much of the criticism was justified. Eventually, friends persuaded her to reconsider her decision and sing again. "There came a time when I couldn't stand it any longer and I just absolutely had to go back to singing," she recalled.

Convinced that she was ready to face a New York audience once more, Boghetti entered her in a contest sponsored by the National Music League in conjunction with Lewisohn Stadium, a huge outdoor amphitheater in Manhattan behind City College. The winning vocalist and instrumentalist would be invited to appear as soloists with the New York Philharmonic Orchestra during its popular summer season at the stadium.

Marian would be competing with some three hundred other contestants, and Boghetti took special pains to get ready for her audition. She visited his

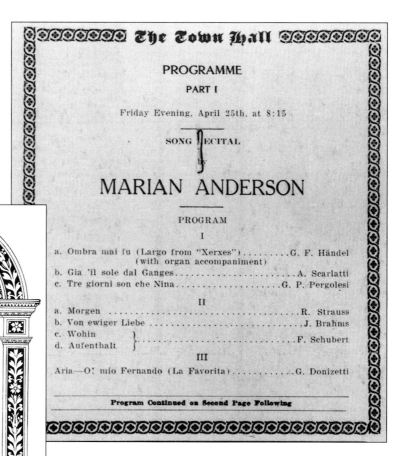

Anderson's disappointing recital at New York's prestigious Town Hall on April 25, 1924, almost ended her singing career.

Philadelphia studio several times a week to rehearse the aria he had asked her to prepare, "O mio Fernando" from Gaetano Donizetti's opera *La Favorita*.

On the day of her audition, Marian took the train to New York, where Boghetti also had a studio, and rehearsed one last time. Then they headed for Aeolian Hall, where the competition to select the winning vocalist was being held.

The contestants with their teachers and accompanists filled the auditorium, while the judges sat by themselves high up in the balcony. They had to listen to as many as a hundred contestants a day over a three-day period, so they didn't waste time. They had a device that made a loud clicking sound up there in the balcony, and when that noisy clicker sounded, the contestant was supposed to stop singing in midpassage and walk off the stage.

Marian was assigned a number—44A. As she waited for her turn, at least six contestants before her launched into "O mio Fernando," the same aria she was to sing. In each case, the dreaded clicker sounded after a minute or two, before the contestant had reached the middle of the aria. Boghetti leaned over and whispered in Marian's ear. No matter what happened, he told her, she must not be intimidated by the clicker. She must continue singing until she reached the difficult trill at the end of the aria, in order to show off the range and power of her voice.

But it wasn't in Marian's nature to defy rules. Silently, she made up her mind that if the clicker sounded, she would stop singing. At last, her number was called. She took her place on the stage, closed her eyes, and began to sing, "with one part of my mind waiting apprehensively for the voice of doom upstairs."

The clicker was silent. She was allowed to sing the complete aria. No other contestant had gone through an entire number. Then a judge called down from the balcony, "Does 44A have another song?" Marian sang an English song, again all the way through. Then the next contestant was summoned.

A few days later, Boghetti phoned Marian in Philadelphia to tell her that she had been chosen as one of sixteen semifinalists. Back in New York for the next phase of the contest, she sang "O mio Fernando" again for the judges, along with two English songs she had prepared. Four vocalists were to be chosen to compete in the final round, but soon after Marian had returned from Aeolian Hall to Boghetti's New York studio, the phone rang. When Boghetti hung up, he shouted, "We have won! There will be no finals!"

The Lewisohn Stadium concert took place on August 26, 1925. Marian's entire family, along with many friends and well-wishers, traveled from Philadelphia to attend. Marian wore a new powder blue dress, "very smart without being gaudy." When the time came for her to appear onstage, "It was a thrill to walk through the aisle made by the musicians and take my place right beside the conductor. As I looked out, there seemed to be a sea of faces; the stadium, I saw, was packed. . . . I will not say that I was not nervous. Perhaps deep down there was the painful memory of the Town Hall fiasco."

An audience of 7,500 people filled Lewisohn Stadium that evening. Marian sang "O mio Fernando," followed by several spirituals, winning enthusiastic applause and, this time, approval from the critics. "A remarkable voice was

$\mathcal{S}$tadium $\mathcal{C}$oncerts

EIGHTH SEASON

The New York Philharmonic Orchestra

110 PLAYERS

LEWISOHN STADIUM
of the
COLLEGE OF THE CITY OF NEW YORK
138th STREET AND AMSTERDAM AVENUE

After competing with 300 other contestants, Marian sang with the New York Philharmonic at Lewisohn Stadium on August 26, 1925.

STADIUM PROGRAMS

(Continued from page 13)

4. Overture, Nocturne and Scherzo from Music for "A Midsummer Night's Dream", ... MENDELSSOHN
5. "Pacific, 231" . . . . HONEGGER
6. Symphonic Poem, "The Preludes" . . . . LISZT

WEDNESDAY EVENING, AUGUST 26th
Soloist: MARIAN ANDERSON, *Contralto* (Stadium Audition Winner)

1. March for Grand Orchestra, Op. 57 . . . . RICHARD STRAUSS
   (First time at the Stadium)
2. Aria, "O, Mio Fernando," from "La Favorita" . . . . DONIZETTI
   MARIAN ANDERSON
3. Two Dances for Orchestra . . . . DEBUSSY
   (A) Sarabande   (B) Danse
   (ORCHESTRATED BY MAURICE RAVEL)
4. Negro Songs and Spirituals
   (a) "Deep River" . . . . H. T. BURLEIGH
   (b) "Heav'n, heav'n" . . . . H. T. BURLEIGH
   (c) "Song of the Heart" . . . . J. H. JOHNSON
   MARIAN ANDERSON
   At the Piano: WILLIAM KING
   INTERMISSION
5. Symphony No. 1, in C minor, Op. 68 . . . . BRAHMS
   I. Un poco sostenuto   III. Un poco allegretto e grazioso
   II. Andante sostenuto   IV. Adagio; Piu Andante; Allegro non troppo, ma con brio
   (Progam continued on page 16)
   THE STEINWAY IS THE OFFICIAL PIANO OF THE STADIUM CONCERTS

Marian Anderson around 1925, when she appeared at Lewisohn Stadium.

heard last night at the Lewisohn Stadium," reported Francis D. Perkins in the *New York Herald-Tribune*. "[Miss Anderson] had given a recital at Town Hall on April 25, 1924, but that had hinted little at the astonishing vocal powers displayed by the young singer last night. . . . It had hardly seemed then the voice in a thousand—or shall we try ten thousand or a hundred thousand?—that it appeared to be last night."

The concert, covered by newspapers around the country, opened the door to more engagements. Marian and Billy King established a pattern of appearances that didn't change much from one year to the next. They toured the southern states early in the year, performed at cities in the Midwest and Northeast during the spring and summer, and also had invitations from Canada and the West Coast. Marian attracted her biggest audiences at black schools and churches in the South. She performed at every major black college, often for several seasons in a row. Billy kept a card file of each place where they appeared, and during the 1920s they accumulated nearly two hundred cards.

Even so, Marian was growing increasingly restless and dissatisfied. She could not find a reliable concert manager who was willing to take on a young black singer, so she and Billy had to make all booking and travel arrangements themselves. The indignities of segregation continued to make travel frustrating and unpleasant. And when Marian performed before predominantly white audiences in the big cities of the Northeast and Midwest, reviewers who praised her voice often commented that she did not handle foreign languages well. She realized that until she understood the subtle nuances of foreign words, and could pronounce them like a native, she could not hope to sing effectively in other languages.

Boghetti coached her in Italian, but she found it difficult to master the German lieder that were an important part of any recital. Once, during a performance when she was singing in German, she forgot some words and improvised others instead. "It was an uncomfortable moment," she recalled. "People were gracious, but the incident disturbed me. It kept haunting me and making me feel that I must find some way to become absolutely sure of my German."

She began to think about studying in Europe. That way, she felt, she could acquire the linguistic skills that would allow her to sing convincingly in languages other than English. And in any case, as she well knew, an American concert singer who did not study and perform successfully abroad couldn't hope to have a distinguished career at home.

Marian's concert fees had been increasing. She and Billy were now getting a total of $350 to $500 an engagement. Her sisters had finished school and were working. And she had persuaded her mother to quit her job as a cleaning lady at Wanamaker's Department Store. "One of the things that made me happiest in my life was that I could tell Mother, who worked hard every day, that she didn't have to work anymore," she recalled. Things were going well enough that she felt she could invest some of her savings in a few months' study in Europe.

"Mother and I discussed the matter at length," she later wrote. "My career needed a fresh impetus, and perhaps a European stamp would help."

Marian (left) *and her mother, Anna, lead a formal procession into a Philadelphia reception during the early 1930s. Throughout her life, Marian turned to her mother for advice and support.*

Marian Anderson in 1936,
after her triumphant return to America.

Four

MARIAN FEVER

*"I knew that I had to test myself as a serious artist
in my own country."*

In the fall of 1927 Marian Anderson sailed for England, armed with letters of introduction and with $1,500 in savings, enough to last for several months. A number of African American performers, among them Roland Hayes, Alberta Hunter, and Josephine Baker, escaping racism in the United States, had enjoyed successful careers in England and France. Some of them, living in London, had promised to help Marian when she arrived.

She was invited to stay at the home of John Payne, a popular American-born actor who had a large London house and often played host to visiting musicians and students. Marian took classes in German and French, studied with a famous teacher of German lieder, and met many people in London's close-knit music community. When she felt she could afford it, she went to concerts where she heard some of the great artists of the time, among them the pianist Arthur Rubinstein and the singers Lily Pons and Elisabeth Schumann.

The highlight of her stay was her appearance, arranged by friends, at London's popular summer concert series the Proms. She sang an aria from Verdi's opera *Don Carlo* along with four spirituals. "There is no doubt that you are rooting for me," she wrote to her mother, ". . . and you've no idea how it helps. . . . [The audience] yelled *more More* while those in the balcony and circle yelled *Bravo* and *stomped* the floor after spirituals. There were lots of bows and encores."

While visiting London in 1927, Anderson (fourth from right) *stayed at the home of John Payne* (second from right), *a popular African American singer and actor who had settled permanently in England.*

Even so, she returned to the United States with no major achievements to show for her absence of nearly a year. Her months abroad had little effect on her career at home. Although she now had a reputable concert manager, the Arthur Judson Agency, to book her appearances, she continued to travel with Billy King much as she always had, performing at black colleges and churches and for the local music organizations and concert series that had always accounted for most of her engagements. Much of America in the 1920s did not open its arms to a black singer performing the classics. "[My] high hopes began to dwindle," Marian recalled. "Progress seemed to have stopped; I had substantially the same circuit of concerts but little more. I was beginning to feel that I was at a standstill."

She hadn't been home very long before she decided that she ought to go back to Europe, this time to Germany, where she could immerse herself in the study of

German lieder. "I knew I must go, and I believed that a way would be found," she recalled.

Her chance came when she was offered a fellowship to study in Germany by the Julius Rosenwald Fund, a foundation that awarded educational grants to African Americans. In June 1930 Marian sailed for Europe again. Settling in Berlin, she roomed with an elderly couple who spoke only German, devoted herself to an intensive study of the language, and began vocal studies with Kurt Johnen, one of the city's best-known teachers.

By October she was confident enough to make her debut in the German capital, but she wasn't well known enough to get financial backing for a full-length

In Berlin in 1931, Anderson studied with Kurt Johnen, a well-known voice coach.

concert. "Accordingly I did what I had never done before and have not done since," she later said. "I put up the money myself. I handed five hundred dollars' worth of American Express checks to [a local concert manager], parting with them with the greatest reluctance, and he arranged a date at the Bachsaal," a famous Berlin concert hall named after Johann Sebastian Bach.

She was understandably nervous. She had risked part of her fellowship money to sing before an audience that knew the words of most German lieder by heart, and she worried that few people would even bother to show up. But when she walked out onto the stage of the Bachsaal that evening, the hall was full. A young Negro contralto was a rarity in German concert life, and many people came out of curiosity. Others in the audience were knowledgeable music lovers and important Berlin critics. Marian, tall, slim, and elegant, with her assured stage presence, sang ten songs in German, an aria in Italian, and several spirituals in English.

Afterward, the concert manager rushed backstage and exclaimed, "I did not know I had such an artist. You are marvelous." And one of the critics wrote, "Her command of our language and our world of feeling was amazing," adding that her "appearance in the Bachsaal caused a sensation."

Offstage, Marian's quiet beauty and unaffected charm had always attracted suitors, and that was the case in Berlin. During her stay two young men vied for her attentions, each ignorant of the other's interest. While she enjoyed the flirtations and romantic intrigue ("I have had a most wonderful time," she confided to a friend. "It was too much I tell you, too much!"), she wasn't interested in a serious involvement.

Orpheus Fisher, the boyfriend from her high school days, still hoped that they could have a future together. He wrote regularly to Marian and complained that she rarely answered his letters. But consumed with her studies and excited by the prospect of additional concerts in Europe, Marian was quite certain that she wasn't ready for marriage. "One gets swept up in a career," she said later, "and one has time for little else."

That fall she was introduced to two music scouts from Scandinavia. Rule Rasmussen, a Norwegian concert manager, and Kosti Vehanen, a Finnish pianist, were traveling through Europe in search of talented performers. They heard Marian at a small recital, and as she sang her first note, Vehanen thought, "From where does this tone come? It was as though the room had begun to vibrate, as though the sound came from under the earth!"

Orpheus Fisher wanted to marry Marian, but she was too busy with her singing career to consider a serious romantic involvement.

Impressed, they invited Marian to give a series of concerts in the Scandinavian countries. No black singer had ever appeared in Scandinavia before, and one with the name Anderson, a very common name in Sweden, was sure to attract attention.

In November and December 1930 Marian Anderson appeared in the capital cities of Oslo, Norway; Stockholm, Sweden; Helsinki, Finland; and Copenhagen, Denmark. Her striking appearance and velvety contralto voice electrified audiences wherever she went, and as word of her performances spread, other cities were added to the tour. The reaction, she felt, "was a mixture of open-mindedness and curiosity. . . . People . . . accepted you as an individual in your own right, judging you for your qualities as a human being and artist and for nothing else. . . . There was an eager warmth in these people that I shall never forget."

By the end of her three-week tour, Anderson had given more than a dozen concerts throughout Scandinavia. She returned to the United States at the end of the year with a renewed sense of confidence and optimism: "The first visit to the north took only a few weeks, but it made a tremendous difference in my life."

She was invited to return, and during the early 1930s she made several triumphant tours of the Scandinavian countries under the management of Helmer Enwall, whose concert bureau was the largest in Scandinavia. With Kosti Vehanen as her accompanist, she appeared nearly everywhere in Sweden, Norway, Finland, and Denmark—in small communities near the Arctic Circle and in every major city—singing always to sold-out houses, wildly enthusiastic audiences, and ecstatic reviews. People stood in line for hours to buy tickets to her recitals. Admirers sent flowers to her hotel. Newspapers ran articles and photographs about her. One Swedish paper called the excitement over her appearances "Marian fever."

Marian Anderson with Helmer Enwall, her Scandinavian concert manager, and Enwall's wife, Therese. The Enwalls became close friends of Marian's, and she spent many holidays at their summer house north of Stockholm.

When she sang for composer Jean Sibelius at his home in Finland, he threw his arms around her, said "My ceiling is much too low for your voice," and called for champagne. Later he dedicated a song, "Solitude," to her. Even the king of Sweden was intrigued enough to attend one of her concerts.

"It was a wonderful time for me," she remembered. "My total earnings were the highest of my career. I sent money home to my family. I bought new evening dresses and clothes for street wear. I purchased a great deal of music, and for the first time I could indulge in the luxury of having it bound in leather."

And yet she never took her popularity for granted. As a guest of the Scandinavian peoples, she made it a point to learn their folk songs in the original languages. And after a performance, when she went back to her hotel room, she would look over the music to see where a certain song, or a passage in a song, could be sung more effectively. "If these people believed in me as an artist," she said, "then I could venture to be a better one."

Her success in Scandinavia was accompanied by acclaim throughout the rest of Europe. She sang in virtually every major European city—in London, Paris, Amsterdam, and Brussels, in Geneva, Vienna, Budapest, and Prague. She toured

Accompanied by Kosti Vehanen, Marian Anderson sings at a 1935 concert in Budapest, Hungary.

Italy, appearing in Turin, Milan, Venice, and Rome, where Crown Princess Marie Jose invited her to give a special performance for her family and guests at the Quirinal Palace. And she traveled twice to the Soviet Union, appearing in Moscow and Leningrad (now St. Petersburg), and in faraway Georgia, Ukraine, and Azerbaijan. During one ten-month period she gave 123 concerts in fifteen different countries, performing a repertoire that included over two hundred songs and arias in German, Italian, English, French, Spanish, Portuguese, Swedish, Finnish, and other languages. Following the tradition established by Roland Hayes and other African American concert vocalists, she concluded each of her programs with a group of spirituals that often moved her audiences to tears.

At the Salzburg Festival in Austria in 1935, the celebrated conductor Arturo Toscanini attended one of her recitals. Afterward, dazzled by Anderson's voice, he went backstage to meet her. Toscanini was perhaps the most famous personality in

Arturo Toscanini. "A voice . . . heard once in a hundred years," declared the famous conductor.

the musical world at that time. "The sight of him caused my heart to leap and throb so violently that I did not hear a word he said," Marian recalled. But others who were present that evening did hear the maestro's words as he took Marian's hand. "A voice like yours," he told her, "is heard once in a hundred years."

Anderson returned to the United States at the end of 1935, ready to begin her first season under the management of Sol Hurok, the renowned international concert promoter, who had signed her to a contract after hearing her sing in Paris. Asked why she did not settle permanently in Europe, where she had enjoyed such success, she replied: "I had gone to Europe to achieve something, to reach for a place as a serious artist, but I never doubted that I must return. I wanted to come home, and I knew that I had to test myself as a serious artist in my own country."

She also had to make what she called "a difficult, even painful decision" before returning home. Kosti Vehanen, her Finnish accompanist, had appeared with her in Scandinavia and throughout Europe, while Billy King had been her accompanist in the United States and a "good and faithful friend" as well. Who should be her accompanist when she returned?

King was understandably upset at the prospect of losing the opportunity to perform with Marian. He argued that the American public, particularly in the South, would not accept a white man as Anderson's accompanist. "You are making the mistake of your life," he wrote to her. "What do you think the reaction all over the United States will be?"

Anderson made her final decision based on her best musical judgment—on the strength of the repertoire and musicianship she had achieved through her years of work with Vehanen. "Because I had been working most recently with Kosti," she said, "I felt more at home with him in the new programs." And so Vehanen sailed with Anderson to America. He continued as her accompanist during both her American and European tours, while Marian and Billy continued as friends. And to everyone's surprise, Anderson's choice of Vehanen as her permanent accompanist caused hardly a ripple of controversy.

She had spent the better part of the past eight years in Europe, and during that time her career in the United States had languished. But word of her "once-in-a-hundred-years" voice had traveled across the Atlantic, and when she appeared in New York's Town Hall on December 30, 1935—eleven years after her disastrous 1924 Town Hall concert—she faced a capacity audience.

Despite warnings that the American public would not accept a white man playing piano for a black singer, Anderson decided to return to America with her Finnish accompanist, Kosti Vehanen. In 1935 they crossed the Atlantic aboard the liner Île de France.

As the curtains parted that evening, the audience murmured in surprise. Instead of walking onto the stage, as was customary, Anderson was already standing onstage, posed with utmost dignity in the curve of the grand piano. Two weeks earlier, on the ship sailing over from Europe, she had slipped on a staircase in rough seas and broken her ankle. A plaster cast, hidden by her black-and-gold brocade gown, covered her left leg from foot to knee.

She had insisted that no public announcement be made concerning her injury. "To tell the audience I was singing despite a broken ankle would smack of searching for pity, and I was not there for pity that night," she recalled. She had limped out onstage with her crutches while the curtains were closed and planted herself securely by the piano. Standing motionless, she captivated an audience that included other well-known singers.

"Let it be said at the outset," critic Howard Taubman wrote in *The New York Times*, "Marian Anderson has returned to her native land one of the great singers of our time. . . . [Her voice] is a contralto of stunning range and volume, managed with suppleness and grace. . . . It was music-making that probed too deep for words. . . . Europe has acclaimed this tall, handsome girl. It is time for her own country to honor her."

She was exhilarated by the rave reviews, but always the self-critical artist, she wasn't satisfied. Back in Philadelphia, she got out her music: "I studied the songs I had sung at Town Hall, examining my singing in retrospect to check where I had not done as I would have liked. . . . Here was a song that should have begun more softly and ended more powerfully. There was another that had not been all of a piece. . . . I resolved to be more careful."

Marian Anderson greets well-wishers after a concert at Carnegie Hall. Directly behind her are her sister Alyse and her mother, Anna.

Anderson now found herself in great demand throughout the United States. She toured the country from coast to coast, performing with some of the great singers, musicians, and conductors of the day. In 1936 she returned to Europe, and twice, in 1937 and 1938, she toured South America, where she was a sensation. During the late 1930s she was heard in living rooms across America as a popular radio performer, appearing on such widely listened-to programs as *The General Motors Hour* and *The Ford Hour*. On the concert stage or over the airwaves, the transcendent quality of her voice touched her audiences deeply. One critic praised "Miss Anderson's power to move her listeners as can no other singer of her generation."

"I have rarely heard a more beautiful and moving voice," said First Lady Eleanor Roosevelt.

In 1936 First Lady Eleanor Roosevelt invited Anderson to sing at the White House for the president, Franklin Delano Roosevelt, and their invited guests. Mrs. Roosevelt also asked Marian's mother, Anna, to attend the small gathering. "The look of happiness and the anticipation on Mrs. Anderson's face are hard to describe," wrote Kosti Vehanen.

After Marian's recital, the first lady took Anna Anderson by the hand and led her over to meet the president. "I shall never forget seeing these two ladies enter the room," Vehanen wrote. "Mrs. Roosevelt's manner was sure and free, as becomes a woman of the world, happy to welcome the mother of America's best-known singer. In all of Mrs. Anderson's being, there was evident the feeling that this was one of the greatest moments in her life. Her face reflected her gratitude and the pride she felt."

The next day, Eleanor Roosevelt described the evening in her nationally syndicated newspaper column, "My Day": "My husband and I had a rare treat Wednesday night in listening to Marian Anderson, a colored contralto, who has made a great success in Europe and this country. She has sung before nearly all the crowned heads, and deserves her great success, for I have rarely heard a more beautiful and moving voice or a more finished artist."

Even so, being welcomed by the White House and applauded by royalty weren't enough to open the doors of the most prestigious auditorium in Washington, D.C.—Constitution Hall.

Marian Anderson sings at the Paris Opera,
December 14, 1937.

Five

BANNED BY THE DAR

"I don't care if she sings from the top
of the Washington Monument, as long as she sings."

Constitution Hall was the largest and finest auditorium in Washington, home to the National Symphony Orchestra and the Washington Opera Company, and host to distinguished visiting orchestras and concert artists. With its brilliant acoustics and nearly 4,000-seat capacity, it was the only hall in the nation's capital that could compare with those in which Marian Anderson had appeared in cities throughout the United States and the world.

The hall had been built as part of the national headquarters of the Daughters of the American Revolution, a patriotic society founded in 1890. Membership was confined to women with at least one ancestor who had aided the cause of the Revolutionary War. The society, active in the preservation and marking of historic sites, was known for its conservative social and political policies. In 1932 the DAR had decreed that "white artists only" would be permitted to appear at Constitution Hall.

Like many American cities during the 1930s, Washington, D.C., with its large black population, was still segregated along racial lines. And yet the laws and customs governing segregation in the nation's capital weren't nearly as strict as those in the cities of the Deep South. While Washington law required separate public schools for black students and white students, recreational facilities and auditoriums often were available to interracial groups after school hours. And while it was customary to require black patrons to sit in separate assigned sections when attending white theaters, this practice was at times overlooked. During the late 1920s and 1930s black and white patrons integrated the audiences of numerous lectures, meetings, and concerts in government auditoriums and in private concert halls.

When Constitution Hall was opened in 1929, DAR officials had set aside a small section of seats in the rear balcony for black patrons. However, the society soon found that it could not enforce this segregated seating policy when black performers appeared in the hall. To avoid mixed seating in the future, the DAR had voted in 1932 to impose a "white artists only" policy. That policy went unchallenged until early January 1939, when the Howard University School of Music applied to book Constitution Hall for an appearance by Marian Anderson.

Constitution Hall, completed in 1929, was the largest and finest auditorium in Washington, D.C.

Members of the DAR and invited dignitaries at the organization's 1924 convention.

Anderson had been singing in Washington ever since her high school days, appearing first at black churches and small black-operated theaters, and later before larger, racially mixed audiences in the auditoriums of black high schools. Starting in the early 1930s her Washington recitals were part of an annual concert series at Howard University, an influential black institution and a training ground for many young black lawyers who would play important roles in the civil rights movement.

By 1936, when Anderson had returned from Europe and was beginning her first season under the management of the famous impresario Sol Hurok, the chapel on the Howard campus, where her recitals were held, was too small to satisfy the growing demand for tickets. A larger auditorium had to be found. Since

Marian Anderson (center) *receives an honorary doctorate of music from Howard University and the congratulations of those attending the ceremony, June 1938.*

black artists were barred from appearing at Constitution Hall, Howard officials decided to schedule Anderson's 1936 concert at Armstrong High School, a black school with a large auditorium. She performed at Armstrong before an integrated audience. Shortly after that concert, Eleanor Roosevelt invited her to sing at the White House.

Anderson appeared at Armstrong High again in 1937, but as the demand for tickets to her performances continued to grow, Howard University rented the still larger downtown Rialto Theater for her 1938 concert. In 1939 the Rialto wasn't available, and the Howard concert series had to find another and even larger location for its most popular event.

Howard officials had applied to the DAR for the use of Constitution Hall back in 1936, believing, perhaps, that the organization would make an exception to its "white artists only" policy for someone with Marian Anderson's reputation. When their request was turned down, they had settled for Armstrong High. In 1939 they applied again for the use of Constitution Hall. Again their request was rejected on the grounds that the hall had a standing policy of not renting concert space to black artists.

This time the university was not willing to back down. Constitution Hall clearly was the most appropriate place in Washington for a concert by Anderson. Howard officials decided to challenge the DAR's restrictive policy, beginning a crucial battle in the campaign to end Jim Crow social practices in the nation's capital.

Howard University Treasurer V. D. Johnston published an open letter in the *Washington Times-Herald,* criticizing the DAR. A few days later the *Times-Herald* ran an editorial titled "We Must Hear Marian Anderson." "[Constitution Hall] stands almost in the shadow of the Lincoln Memorial, but the Great Emancipator's sentiments about 'race, creed or previous condition of servitude' are not shared by the Daughters," the paper said. "Prejudice rules to make the Capital of the Nation ridiculous in the eyes of all cultured people." The newspaper called on Congress to build a federal auditorium in Washington that would be free of racial discrimination. Meanwhile. a small group of friends and associates, people of power and influence who believed in equal rights, was planning a campaign to marshal public opinion. Among them were Walter White, executive secretary of the National Association for the Advancement of Colored People; Secretary of the Interior Harold L. Ickes, a strong advocate of racial justice; and Eleanor Roosevelt, the first lady.

Interior Secretary Harold L. Ickes (left), First Lady Eleanor Roosevelt, and NAACP chief Walter White teamed up to protest the DAR's ban and to find a suitable site for a Marian Anderson concert.

Ickes wrote to Mrs. Henry M. Robert, Jr., president general of the DAR, saying, "This is such an astounding discrimination against equal rights that I am loath to believe that the Daughters of the American Revolution should invoke such a rule." Speaking for the NAACP, White also wrote to President General Robert. "Barring a world famed artist because of color from a building named by the Daughters of the American Revolution 'Constitution Hall' violates the very spirit and purpose of the immortal document after which the hall is named," he said.

At White's suggestion, telegrams were sent out to prominent members of the musical community, asking them to protest the DAR's ban on black performers. Within days leading performers and conductors began to telegraph their disapproval to the DAR. Kirsten Flagstad, the internationally celebrated Norwegian soprano who was appearing with New York's Metropolitan Opera, expressed the views of many others when she wired: "As a foreigner in America, I have always been impressed by the freedom and democracy in this country. I therefore am greatly surprised to learn that the use of Constitution Hall in Washington has been refused for a concert to my fellow-artist, Marian Anderson."

But Mrs. Robert refused to budge. Constitution Hall was not available for a concert by Marian Anderson.

Convinced that the DAR would not reverse its policy, Howard University applied to the Washington, D.C., Board of Education for the use of the Central High School auditorium, one of the city's largest school auditoriums. But when the School Board met, it backed away from what had become an incendiary controversy. Since Central was a white high school, the Board turned down the request and recommended the use of the Armstrong High auditorium instead.

The School Board's decision was front-page news in every Washington paper. As public opposition to the racial ban against Anderson mounted, representatives of some two dozen local and national organizations formed the interracial Marian Anderson Citizens' Committee. Members of the group picketed the Board of Education and collected several thousand signatures on a petition denouncing the board's action "as contrary to the spirit of democracy, and as a backward step in the development of interracial goodwill in the District of Columbia."

The Committee called a mass protest meeting to "defend our democratic right to hear Marian Anderson sing," and sent out a call for telegrams supporting an Anderson concert. One of the first people to respond was Eleanor Roosevelt, who wired: "I regret extremely that Washington is to be deprived of hearing Marian Anderson, a great artist."

Mrs. Roosevelt, in her day the most outspoken of presidents' wives, had worked tirelessly since coming to Washington to promote racial equality. A few weeks earlier she had refused to accept a segregated seating pattern at a meeting of the Southern Conference for Human Welfare in Birmingham, Alabama. When she arrived at the auditorium with a friend, black educator Mary McLeod Bethune, she was told that blacks and whites were not allowed to sit together at public gatherings in Birmingham. A local law required them to sit on opposite sides of an auditorium's center aisle. Eleanor Roosevelt refused to obey the segregation rule. When the police told her that she was violating the law, she demanded that a chair be placed directly in the center aisle, and she sat there.

Now, in Washington, Mrs. Roosevelt conferred with Walter White of the NAACP and with Howard University officials on how she could best use her influence as first lady to demonstrate her support for Marian Anderson. To be most effective, she felt, her actions must be seen as a response to an important *national* issue, not just a local controversy. Eleanor's ancestors had fought in the Revolutionary War. She was a member in good standing of the DAR. But she decided she could not remain a member of an organization that practiced a racially restrictive policy, and she resigned in protest. "You had an opportunity to lead in an enlightened way," she wrote to DAR President General Robert, "and it seems to me that your organization has failed." The next day, Mrs. Roosevelt announced her resignation in her nationally syndicated newspaper column, focusing worldwide attention on the controversy.

"I have been debating in my mind for some time a question which I have had to debate with myself once or twice before in my life," she wrote in "My Day." "The question is, if you belong to an organization and disapprove of an action which is typical of a policy, should you resign or is it better to work for a changed point of view within the organization? . . . In this case I belong to an organization in which I can do no active work. They have taken an action which has been widely talked of in the press. To remain as a member implies approval of that action, and therefore I am resigning."

News of Mrs. Roosevelt's resignation was splashed across the front pages of more than four hundred newspapers from San Francisco to New York City. She wasn't the first woman to resign from the DAR over this issue, but by placing her

MRS. ROOSEVELT QUITS D.A.R.

★ PHILADELPHIA EDITION ★
Pittsburgh Courier
★★AMERICA'S★★ ★★★BEST★★★ ★★★WEEKLY★★★

Philadelphia
Office:
2041 W.
Columbia Ave
Phone:
Stevenson 4841

10¢
PER COPY
EVERYWHERE

VOL. XXX—No. 9   SATURDAY, MARCH 4, 1939   PRICE—TEN CENTS

REBUKED DAR?

Mrs. Franklin D. Roosevelt
who strongly hinted at a press
conference Monday that she had
resigned from the Daughters of
the American Revolution because
of its ban against Marian Anderson.

PRESIDENT'S WIFE RAPS EXCLUSION OF MISS ANDERSON

WASHINGTON, March 2—Mrs. Franklin D. Roosevelt
hinted strongly Monday at a press conference that she
had resigned her membership in the Daughters of the
American Revolution in protest against the bar which
that organization raised at Con-
stitution Hall against the celebrated singer, Marian Anderson.

The First Lady did not say specifically that she had resigned from
the D.A.R. but comment in her
column, "My Day," and her an-
swers to reporters at the conference were almost proof positive
that the D.A.R. was meant.

In her column, and at the conference, she commented on having
been faced recently with the di-
lemma of staying in an organization to fight a policy of which she
did not approve or resigning from
the organization. She declared she
had made up her mind to resign
because she was not active enough
in the organization to fight it out.

She stated: "I belong to an organization in which I can do no
active work. It has taken an action which has been widely-talked
of in the press. To remain as a
member implies approval of that
action, and therefore I am resigning."

When asked directly if it were
from the D.A.R. she had resigned, she countered with the sugges-
tions that the inquiry be taken
to the D.A.R. itself for response.

(Continued on Page Four)

STORM CENTER

Eleanor Roosevelt's resignation from the DAR made headlines across the country.

political influence and personal popularity on the line, she provoked national publicity and outrage toward an act of conspicuous racism. "Of course people became aroused when Mrs. Roosevelt resigned," Marian Anderson later observed. "She was a powerful person. People lived according to her example."

Meanwhile, the Washington School Board decided to reverse itself. It offered to grant Anderson the use of Central High for this one concert only, on condition that her appearance at a white school would not be considered a precedent and that no further applications from Anderson be submitted. When Howard University refused to accept any such restriction, the Superintendent of Schools promptly withdrew the offer.

In the midst of all this controversy, Walter White and Sol Hurok began to discuss the possibility of a free outdoor concert by Anderson. At first they thought of staging the concert in the small public park directly across the street from Constitution Hall. But White wasn't comfortable with the idea. "I think it would be undignified and too much like a small boy thumbing his nose at the back of a larger boy who has beaten him up," he said.

Marian Anderson with her American concert manager, Sol Hurok, photographed in Europe.

Then they came up with a better idea. A free concert at the Lincoln Memorial would attract thousands of people, far more than any auditorium could hold, and would send a powerful message of defiance against the injustice of bigotry and racial discrimination.

The Lincoln Memorial was administered by the U.S. Department of the Interior, so Walter White spoke to Oscar Chapman, the assistant secretary. Chapman went immediately to his boss, who happened to be Interior Secretary Ickes. Excited by the idea, Ickes hurried over to the White House to catch

President Roosevelt, who was preparing to leave town that day. Roosevelt had been advised of the plan by his wife, Eleanor, who had persuaded him to delay his departure until he could speak to Ickes. "I don't care if she sings from the top of the Washington Monument," the president told Ickes, "as long as she sings."

Later that afternoon, at a crowded press conference, Ickes announced that the Lincoln Memorial would be the site of a concert by Marian Anderson on Easter Sunday, April 9, 1939.

Marian Anderson to give free concert in Capital

(Special Dispatch to the Philadelphia DAILY NEWS)

NEW YORK, Feb. 28.—With the declaration that Marian Anderson, famed Philadelphia-born Negro contralto, had been denied rental of Constitution hall, Washington, on April 8 and 10 as well as April 9, a rented date, S. Hurok, manager of the singing star, today revealed that she will give a free, open-air concert in Washington on the latter date.

His assertion came in reply to an "explanation" by Mrs. Frank L. Nason, registrar general of the Daughters of the American Revolution, owners of Constitution hall, that Miss Anderson had been refused the auditorium because it was already rented for the 9th—Easter Sunday—to the National Broadcasting Co. orchestra.

Open to 'White Artists'

"That is what they told us when we made application for April 9," Hurok said. "Later, we learned on good authority that April 8 and 10 were open to 'white artists.' We

MARIAN ANDERSON
Cheered in Frisco

applied for either of these dates

Marion Anderson To Give Open-Air Capital Concert

CONTINUED FROM PAGE THREE

Constitution hall, if a police permit can be obtained.

Charter Special Trains

"When we plan a thing, we go through with it," he said. "We are chartering a special train to take people from New York and Pennsylvania to Washington for the concert."

Hurok said he believed the D. A. R. was "just trying to find an excuse."

"You notice Mrs. Robert isn't saying anything," he said.

He referred to Mrs. Henry A. Robert, president general of the D. A. R., who is in Phoenix, Ariz.

D. Roosevelt from "a certain organization"—the D. A. R., everyone understands.

Lauds Mrs. Roosevelt

The action of the President's wife was hailed by Miss Anderson, in San Francisco, as evidence that she "seems to be the one who really comprehends the true meaning of democracy."

pear in the capital of her native land.

Hurok angrily took issue with the D. A. R. statement that the permit was denied because the hall was rented.

He said that despite the D. A. R's rejection, followed by the school board refusal to permit Miss An-

Easter Sunday, April 9, 1939: Marian Anderson and her mother, Anna,
lay a wreath at the Lincoln Memorial on the day of Anderson's historic concert.

Six

SINGING TO THE NATION

"I sang, I don't know how."

Marian Anderson was hurrying to the theater in San Francisco when she passed a newsstand and a headline caught her eye: MRS. ROOSEVELT TAKES STAND: RESIGNS FROM DAR. "I was on my way to the concert hall for my performance and couldn't stop to buy a paper," she recalled. "I did not get one until after the concert, and I honestly could not conceive that things had gone so far."

The controversy over Constitution Hall had started while Anderson was on a nationwide tour, and as she said later, she wasn't fully aware of what was happening until she spotted that San Francisco headline. At first she was very upset. "Music to me means so much, such beautiful things," she recalled, "it seemed impossible that you could find people who would curb you, stop you, from doing a thing which is beautiful."

Back at her San Francisco hotel she found a telegram from Sol Hurok, informing her of plans for a huge outdoor concert. Later, at Hurok's suggestion, she made a brief statement to reporters in the hotel lobby: "I am not surprised at Mrs. Roosevelt's action because she seemed to me to be one who really comprehended the true meaning of democracy. I am shocked beyond words to be barred from the capital of my own country after having appeared in almost every other capital in the world."

As Anderson continued with her scheduled tour, the furor over Constitution Hall "seemed to increase and follow me wherever I went." Reporters and photographers were waiting for her at every stop with a barrage of questions: "Do you feel insulted by this refusal?" "What is your attitude toward all this?" "What do you intend to do?" But she was reluctant to speak out. "I did not want to talk," she recalled, "and I particularly did not want to say anything about the DAR. As I have made clear, I did not feel that I was designed for hand-to-hand combat, and I did not wish to make statements that I would later regret."

Anderson was not a person who enjoyed controversy or welcomed confrontations. Rather, she was inclined to be generous in her judgments of others. "I was sorry for the people who had precipitated the affair," she later said. "I felt that their behavior stemmed from a lack of understanding. . . . Could I have erased the bitterness, I would have done so gladly." She knew that many DAR members disagreed with the organization's official policy, and she did not want to condemn the entire group.

As she traveled across the country, plans for the Lincoln Memorial concert were moving forward. The National Park Service, a bureau of the Department of the Interior, prepared to handle the huge crowd that was expected. Arrangements were made for press coverage, for sound amplification, and for a coast-to-coast radio hookup that would broadcast the concert to the nation. For the first time in history a grand piano was carried up the Lincoln Memorial steps. Meanwhile, eighty-five national and local organizations, and more than three hundred prominent individuals, signed on as sponsors of the "Freedom Concert," as it was now called. A printed program, featuring lines from the Gettysburg Address, would be distributed by Boy Scouts, white and black, who circulated through the crowd.

Anderson had agreed to the concert, but not without hesitation and doubts. "I said yes, but the yes did not come easily or quickly. I don't like a lot of show, and one could not tell in advance what direction the affair would take. . . . The idea was sound, but it could not be comfortable to me as an individual. . . . [Yet] I could see that my significance as an individual was small in this affair. I had become, whether I liked it or not, a symbol, representing my people. I had to appear."

On Easter Sunday morning, April 9, accompanied by her mother and sisters, Marian rode the train from Philadelphia to Washington's Union Station. Since no hotel would take them, they had been invited to stay at the Washington home of

Howard University and Associated Sponsors

PRESENT

MARIAN ANDERSON

AT

THE LINCOLN MEMORIAL

IN

WASHINGTON

Sunday, April 9, 1939

FIVE O'CLOCK

"Fourscore and seven years ago our fathers brought forth on this continent a new nation, conceived in liberty and dedicated to the proposition that all men are created equal."

ABRAHAM LINCOLN.

Program

America

Aria, "O, Mio Fernando" from "La Favorita"................................*Donizetti*

Ave Maria..*Schubert*

INTERMISSION

Gospel Train...*Burleigh*

Trampin'..*Boatner*

My Soul is Anchored in the Lord...*Florence Price*

At the piano..KOSTI VEHANEN

The printed program for the Lincoln Memorial concert featured a line from Lincoln's Gettysburg Address.

64

Gifford Pinchot, the former governor of Pennsylvania. Early that afternoon, Marian and her accompanist, Kosti Vehanen, were driven to the Lincoln Memorial for a brief preconcert visit. The crowd had not yet started to arrive. They tried out the piano and examined the public address system, a battery of six microphones that would broadcast the event to those present at the Memorial and also to the national radio audience.

Later that day, shortly before the concert was scheduled to begin, Anderson and Vehanen returned to the Memorial in a handsome limousine with a motorcycle escort. Police were waiting to lead them from the car through a passageway that other officers kept open in the dense crowd. Marian had never felt as nervous as she did now: "My heart leaped wildly, and I could not talk. I even wondered whether I would be able to sing."

Entering the monument, they were taken to a small room where Interior Secretary Ickes was waiting. He went over the program with them. Then it was time to go out before the crowd.

Kosti Vehanen went first, moving to the piano to fasten down the music against the brisk afternoon breeze: "When I saw the immense crowd of seventy-five thousand people, then looked at the Steinway piano, I had a feeling that it would be of little use to begin to play, for I was sure that no one could possibly hear it. I also felt how really small a person seems when facing such a gathering, which stretched so far that I could scarcely see the end."

Then Marian was led to her seat on the green-carpeted platform of the Memorial by New York congresswoman Caroline O'Day and Assistant Secretary of the Interior Oscar Chapman. "No member of that audience will ever forget the sight of Miss Anderson emerging from a small anteroom beside [the] statue of Lincoln," Walter White remembered. "She was apparently calm, but those of us who knew her were aware of the great [agitation] beneath her serene exterior."

On the platform behind her, filling the two hundred places that had been reserved for distinguished guests, sat members of Congress, Supreme Court justices, and high-ranking government officials, along with Marian's mother, Anna, and her sisters, Ethel May and Alyse. Across from the elevated platform where Anderson was to stand as she sang was another platform for the film crews that would record the event. And nearby were countless photographers with their cameras at the ready.

The first name among the prominent sponsors listed in the program was "Mrs. Franklin D. Roosevelt," but Eleanor had decided that it was better not to attend. As the most famous, and controversial, woman in America, she did not want to draw attention to herself and upstage Marian Anderson.

Interior Secretary Ickes stepped up to the bank of microphones. "Genius draws no color line," he said. "She has endowed Marian Anderson with such voice as lifts any individual above his fellows, as is a matter of exultant pride to any race. . . . We are grateful to Miss Anderson for coming here to sing for us today."

Interior Secretary Harold L. Ickes greets Marian Anderson before introducing her to an outdoor audience of some 75,000 people.

Anderson rose from her seat. She wore a mink coat and a bright orange-and-yellow scarf about her neck, and she was bareheaded. Drawing her coat closely around her shoulders against the wind, she moved toward the microphones. "She looked regal and dignified as she came forward with slow steps," Vehanen remembered. "When she came to the place where the steps began to descend, she stopped for a moment as she gazed over the enormous gathering of people. Her breath seemed to leave her for that fleeting moment, but I think that those who were privileged to see her at that time were much more moved than she was."

Anderson faced the now hushed and expectant crowd that stretched across the Mall from the base of the Lincoln Memorial all the way to the Washington Monument. Directly behind her, the great Lincoln Memorial was filled with shadow in the late-afternoon light. And the statue of Lincoln looked almost ready to speak.

"There seemed to be people as far as the eye could see," Anderson recalled. "I had a feeling that a great wave of good will poured out from these people, almost engulfing me. And when I stood up to sing . . . I felt for a moment as though I were choking. For a desperate second I thought that the words, well as I knew them, would not come. I sang, I don't know how."

"My feelings were so deep that I have never forgotten it, and I don't think until I leave this earth I will ever forget it," recalled opera and theater performer Todd Duncan. "Number one, I never have been so proud to be an American. Number two, I never have been so proud to be an American Negro. And number three, I never felt such pride [as] in seeing this Negro woman stand up there with this great regal dignity and sing.

"In back of me were the Tidal Basin and Washington Monument. Under my feet was the grass. To the side of me the walls were beautiful trees. The ceiling was the sky. And in front of me were those wonderful majestic stairs going up to the Lincoln Memorial. And there stood Miss Anderson. . . . The highlight of that day were the first words that she sang."

Closing her eyes, Marian Anderson began to sing, and her thrilling contralto voice carried across the Mall, touching every person who had come to hear her. Her opening number was "America," and the words "sweet land of liberty" poured from her almost as a prayer:

My country, 'tis of thee,
Sweet land of liberty,
To thee we sing;
Land where my fathers died,
Land of the Pilgrims' pride,
From every mountain-side
Let Freedom ring!

She did not use the word "I" as she sang. In her rendition "Of thee I sing" was replaced by "*To* thee *we* sing."

Then she sang "O mio Fernando," the aria that had won her the Lewisohn Stadium contest fourteen years earlier, followed by Schubert's "Ave Maria." After a brief intermission she sang three spirituals: "Gospel Train," "Trampin'," and "My Soul Is Anchored in the Lord," and finally, as an encore, she ended with another spiritual, "Nobody Knows the Trouble I See," a gentle lamentation that brought tears to the eyes of many in that hushed audience. "I have never heard such a voice," Ickes wrote in his diary.

As the last notes of the spiritual faded away, while the crowd was still under the spell of her voice, Anderson raised her hand and spoke a few words: "I am so overwhelmed," she said, "I just can't talk. I can't tell you what you have done for me today. I thank you from the bottom of my heart again and again."

Then the spell was broken as great numbers of people, stirred by their own emotions, roared their acclaim and rushed toward Anderson to offer congratulations and good wishes, threatening to mob her. Walter White pushed his way to a microphone and pleaded with the crowd not to create a panic.

"As I did so, but with indifferent success, a single figure caught my eye in the mass of people below which seemed one of the most important and touching symbols of the occasion. It was a slender black girl dressed in somewhat too garishly hued Easter finery. Hers was not the face of one who had been the beneficiary of much education or opportunity. Her hands were particularly noticeable as she thrust them forward and upward, trying desperately, though she was some distance from Miss Anderson, to touch the singer. They were hands that despite their youth had known only the dreary work of manual labor. Tears streamed down the girl's dark face. Her hat was askew, but in her eyes flamed hope bordering on ecstasy. Life which had been none too easy for her now held out greater hope because one who was also colored and who, like herself, had known poverty, privation, and prejudice, had, by her genius, gone a long way toward conquering bigotry. If Marian Anderson could do it, the girl's eyes seemed to say, then I can, too."

As Walter White urged the surging crowd to stay back, the police were rushing Anderson back inside the Memorial. Even there well-wishers almost overwhelmed her, until finally the police were able to clear a passageway through the crowd and escort the singer to a waiting car.

For the rest of Marian Anderson's life, wherever she traveled and sang, people would come backstage after a performance and say, "You know, I was at that Easter concert."

*First Lady Eleanor Roosevelt presents Marian Anderson
with the NAACP's Spingarn Medal, July 2, 1939.*

Seven

BREAKING BARRIERS

"The essential point about wanting to appear in [Constitution Hall] was that I wanted to do so because I felt I had that right as an artist."

The Lincoln Memorial concert made both musical and civil rights history. Thanks to the coast-to-coast radio hookup, millions of people heard Marian Anderson sing that day. Her voice was carried into hamlets and farmhouses far from any concert hall, and newspapers across the country featured the concert as a front-page story. A headline in the *Norfolk Journal and Guide* read: MARIAN ANDERSON THRILLS AMERICA.

The concert is recognized today as a milestone in the struggle for equal rights. It helped create the format of the modern civil rights demonstration, and it established the Lincoln Memorial as moral high ground for generations of protesters.

The NAACP, the civil rights organization most closely identified with the concert, reaped substantial rewards. Within twelve months its membership doubled and contributions to the organization skyrocketed. Anderson, who had not been associated with any civil rights group, now committed herself to the NAACP and became one of its leading fundraisers.

Eleanor Roosevelt learned a valuable lesson from the Constitution Hall controversy. In 1939 she was just beginning to use her "My Day" newspaper column as her own political forum, where she could express her personal ideas and convictions. The column announcing her resignation from the DAR triggered a worldwide reaction and demonstrated the powerful impact Mrs. Roosevelt could have when she spoke out on a political or social issue. She received more mail supporting her resignation than on any other issue she discussed that year. And she continued to use her newspaper column, along with her lectures, radio talks, and press conferences, to publicize her views on social justice.

Two months after the Lincoln Memorial concert, Marian Anderson was invited back to the White House to sing for the visiting king and queen of England. The state dinner at which she appeared was the most select and glamorous social event of the Roosevelt years. Anderson sang the Schubert "Ave Maria" and two spirituals. Afterward, she, along with the other guests, was introduced to the royal couple, King George VI and Queen Elizabeth, and she had a chance to chat briefly with Mrs. Roosevelt. Her participation in the event was the artistic high point of the evening and an unspoken rebuke to the snobbery and prejudice that had excluded her from Constitution Hall.

Later that summer, Anderson and Mrs. Roosevelt met again at the annual conference of the NAACP in Richmond, Virginia, where Marian was honored with the Spingarn Medal, awarded annually "for the highest or noblest achievement by an American Negro during the preceding year or years." An overflow audience of more than five thousand people attended the ceremony and watched Anderson receive the prestigious medal from the hands of the first lady. "It must be tremendously gratifying to feel that you have won out over very great difficulties," Mrs. Roosevelt said.

Marian Anderson was now one of America's most sought after singers. She toured more widely than ever, giving as many as eighty or ninety concerts a year. Kosti Vehanen had retired to his home in Finland. He was replaced as Anderson's accompanist by Franz Rupp, a Jewish pianist who had fled from Nazi Germany with his family after Adolf Hitler came to power.

During World War II (1941–1945), in addition to her regularly scheduled concerts, Anderson sang for servicemen and -women at military bases and hospitals across the country. And she gave many benefit performances to aid wartime causes. One of those benefits took place in Washington, D.C.—at Constitution Hall.

Soon after the war started, the DAR announced a series of concerts to raise funds for war relief. As a gesture of compromise and goodwill, the Daughters invited Marian Anderson to give the opening concert, a benefit for the United China Relief Fund. She accepted on condition that the audience be completely unsegregated, and after some hesitation the DAR agreed. For the first time in its

Franz Rupp, a refugee from Nazi Germany, became Anderson's new accompanist in 1940. He remained with her for twenty-five years.

Singing to the troops at Fort Logan Air Force Base in Colorado during World War II.

history, the organization permitted a concert to be held in Constitution Hall with no segregation of any kind in the seating arrangements.

Anderson's appearance on January 7, 1943, was a gala event. The Chinese ambassador to the United States attended, along with prominent government officials and civil rights leaders. Eleanor Roosevelt was there, as she reported in her newspaper column:

"Last night I attended the Marian Anderson concert, given for Chinese relief. As every seat was filled in Constitution Hall, I am quite sure it was a successful

Walking down the steps of Constitution Hall in the snow after Anderson's benefit concert for the China Relief Fund, January 7, 1943. From left: impresario Sol Hurok, accompanist Franz Rupp, Marian Anderson, and traveling manager Isaac A. Jofe.

financial undertaking. Miss Anderson's program was beautiful and she was certainly most enthusiastically received. It was a significant evening not only from the artistic point of view but from the social point of view."

"The essential point about wanting to appear in the hall was that I wanted to do so because I felt I had that right as an artist," Anderson said later. And she added: "When I finally walked onto the stage of Constitution Hall, I felt no different than I had in other halls. There was no sense of triumph. I felt it was a beautiful concert hall, and I was very happy to sing in it."

The year 1943 also marked a milestone in Marian's personal life. Dedicated to her career, she had put off marriage until she was well into her forties. Finally, she gave in and said yes to Orpheus Fisher, who had been courting her tirelessly since their high school days. "We knew that someday we would be married," she said. Their wedding, a small private ceremony, took place at the Bethel Methodist Church near Danbury, Connecticut.

They wanted to find a country house close to New York City, but in 1943 the color line was still a barrier. Orpheus (known as King to family and close friends) was light skinned enough to pass for white, but the moment he told a real estate agent that he was married to Marian Anderson and that he himself was black, the property suddenly would be taken off the market. He said that he traveled more than 10,000 miles in New York, New Jersey, and Connecticut before finding the hundred-acre property near Danbury that they were finally able to buy, a rambling old farmhouse set among meadows and woods.

They named the property Marianna Farm, combining Marian's name and her mother's, and stocked the place with a collection of farm animals that included horses and cows, chickens, pigs, and sheep. Orpheus, a professional architect, remodeled their house, designed and built a separate studio for Marian, and dammed up a small brook to make a swimming hole. For years Marianna Farm provided a welcome refuge for Marian when she returned from a concert tour. "[Our marriage] was worth waiting for," she said. "King and I have had some lovely times together."

They had planned to have a family, but with the continuing demands of Marian's career, they put that off, too. "When I see other people with children I wonder whether our decision was right," she said years later. "I admire the women in my profession who manage to sustain singing careers and raise families. Perhaps I should have been more daring."

Married at last in 1943, Marian Anderson and Orpheus Fisher are seen here leaving a concert in the early 1950s. "Marriage was worth waiting for," she said.

Marianna Farm near Danbury, Connecticut.

After World War II, Anderson continued to tour extensively in the United States. She performed as a soloist with many of the nation's leading orchestras and became immensely popular with radio audiences, appearing regularly on *The Bell Telephone Hour*, a classical program broadcast weekly over the NBC network. Meanwhile, she returned several times to Europe, toured South America and the West Indies, and was one of the first Western artists to appear in Japan after the war. In 1955 she performed in Israel and was particularly moved by her visit to Jerusalem and other sites in the Holy Land. And in 1957 the U.S. State Department sent her as a goodwill ambassador on a ten-week tour of India and

Anderson's 1957 goodwill tour for the U.S. State Department took her to twelve Asian countries. This photo was taken in Rangoon, Burma (now Myanmar). Included in the party were Isaac A. Jofe *(second from left),* Orpheus Fisher *(third from left),* Franz Rupp *(fourth from right), and* Marian Anderson *(second from right).*

the Far East. Accompanied by a CBS television crew that filmed the tour, she visited twelve countries, singing in concert halls, meeting heads of state, and making informal visits to schools, churches, and local organizations. In South Vietnam she was greeted by a group of schoolchildren who sang "Getting to Know You," from the musical *The King and I.* The children in the front row wore big straw hats with music sheets attached to them, so the children in the row behind could read the English lyrics.

Back home, while Anderson was greeted everywhere as a celebrity, she still felt the sting of racism as she traveled back and forth across the country on concert tours. Her travel arrangements were made by her manager and his staff, who tried to shield her from embarrassment and discomfort. They didn't tell her of the difficulties they sometimes had in making reservations. "I look at the itinerary, see that I am scheduled to stay at a certain hotel in a certain city, and sense that an exception has been made," she wrote in her autobiography in 1956. "It is better not to know for sure. . . . I have a performance to give, and if my feelings are divided I cannot do my best. . . . If I suspect that an exception is being made for me I go into the hotel not with triumph but out of necessity."

Marian Anderson, her accompanist, and her traveling manager are greeted by a local welcoming committee in the late 1940s. Second from left is Franz Rupp; third from left is Isaac A. Jofe.

In one northern city, Anderson was able to stay at the best hotel when she was in town for a performance, but only because her manager had made special arrangements. "She didn't register or come anywhere near the desk," said the hotel manager. "She went right up the elevator to her room, and no one knew she was around."

"Somebody doesn't always come right up to you and say, 'You can't have this, you can't have that,'" she told an interviewer. "It's just as though there's a hair that blows across your face. Nobody sees it, but it's there and you can feel it." But at times somebody did come right up, especially in the South, where her mere presence created a challenge to the tradition of Jim Crow segregation.

On one visit to a southern city, Anderson, who was traveling with her accompanist and manager, found a big welcoming committee when they arrived at the train station. "I was presented with flowers, while photographers from the paper took pictures," she later said. "Then I was interviewed. Finally we were able to leave."

The welcoming ceremony had taken place on the station platform. When everyone reached the door to go through the station to the automobiles waiting on the other side, a uniformed officer, seeing Anderson, barred the doorway with his arm and said, "She can't come through this way. This goes to the white waiting room. She'll have to go through the other side."

Anderson's accompanist, Franz Rupp, and her traveling manager, Isaac Jofe, who were both white, started to protest: "But I stopped them; I didn't want a scene. Then they wanted to go with me, but the official wouldn't permit that either. In the end, the members of the hospitality committee, the photographers, the press, Franz and Jofe, all waited for me by the cars, while I went around to the Negroes' waiting room, through that, and out to join the group."

Early in the 1950s black community leaders in the South began to organize boycotts of concerts and public events that imposed segregated seating. Anderson and other prominent performers were urged to announce publicly that they would no longer appear before segregated audiences. "I believe that the time has come," said black educator Mary McLeod Bethune, "when people like Marian Anderson and others who believe in the complete annihilation of segregation and discrimination should make the public announcement that they will not appear before any segregated audience."

Until then, Anderson and her concert managers had been willing to compromise with established laws and customs in the South. She had always welcomed the opportunity to appear before an audience that wanted to hear her sing, particularly where large numbers of blacks were included. Her solution was to insist on vertical seating—an imaginary line drawn from the front of an auditorium to the topmost balcony, giving both races separate but equal seating opportunities.

But as she listened to the black community's mounting demands for equal rights, she was ready to take a firm stand against segregated audiences of any

Jim Crow segregation signs persisted in some places well into the 1960s.

kind. Vertical seating was a compromise she was no longer willing to make. "I was never very happy about singing in halls where segregation was practiced," she said later. "[Finally] I decided that I had had enough, and I made it a rule that I would not sing where there was segregation."

The times were changing, and Marian Anderson was helping them change. In 1952 the "white artists only" clause was removed from Constitution Hall contracts. From then on, Anderson and other black performers began to appear regularly in the hall, and segregation was no longer an issue.

In 1955 Anderson broke one of the last remaining barriers to black singers in America. Thirty years after her New York debut (and eight years after Jackie Robinson broke the color line in professional baseball), she became the first African American to be a soloist at New York's Metropolitan Opera, an honor accorded her (and the opera company) when she was well past the age at which singers normally make operatic debuts. She sang the role of the sorceress Ulrica in Giuseppe Verdi's *Un Ballo in Maschera* (*A Masked Ball*). When the curtain rose to reveal Anderson sitting before a steaming cauldron, mixing the witch's brew in the darkness of Ulrica's cave, the audience burst into a standing ovation that lasted nearly five minutes before the scene could begin.

Her debut at the Metropolitan Opera, as the first black soloist to perform there in its seventy-one-year history, paved the way for literally hundreds of other singers of color to appear at the Met and at major opera houses in the United States. "It was a tremendous experience for me," Marian said later. "It was so joyful. I only wished that it had come earlier in life when I might have been able to bring more to it."

"Looking back," she remembered, "I see stretching behind me year after year of singing, traveling, packing, unpacking, rehearsing, and studying." And traveling was no simple matter. On the road for six or seven months a year, she toured with a radio and phonograph, a sewing machine, an iron and ironing board, cameras, and as many as twenty bags to hold her gowns and clothes suitable for different climates. Her tours of the United States and Canada alone took her to more than 600 cities, where she performed to over 6 million listeners in more than 1500 auditoriums.

Occasionally, she crossed paths with Eleanor Roosevelt, another perpetual traveler, and they would enjoy a brief visit before going their separate ways. Once, when Anderson was occupying the dressing room of an auditorium where she was to perform, the stage manager told her that Mrs. Roosevelt, who was on a lecture

Metropolitan Opera manager Rudolph Bing asked Marian Anderson to sing with the celebrated New York City opera company, breaking the last barrier to black concert singers in America.

Marian Anderson as the sorceress Ulrica in Giuseppe Verdi's opera A Masked Ball.

Marian Anderson and Eleanor Roosevelt at the Eleanor Roosevelt Center in New York, October 1960.

tour, would occupy the same dressing room two days later. Before leaving, Marian left a greeting for Eleanor, written in soap on the dressing-room mirror. The two women remained lifelong friends, and their correspondence continued until Eleanor's death in 1962.

During her career, Anderson sang twice more on the steps of the Lincoln Memorial: in 1952 at memorial services for her old comrade in arms Harold Ickes, and again in 1963 at the historic Civil Rights March on Washington, at which Martin Luther King, Jr., delivered his eloquent "I Have a Dream" speech before 200,000 peaceful demonstrators. Standing before the giant statue of Lincoln, as she had a quarter century earlier, Anderson sang "He's Got the Whole World in His Hands," and her voice, though diminished by age, was still powerful enough to carry to the farthest reaches of the Reflecting Pool.

Over the years she was showered with awards, tributes, and honorary degrees. She served as a U.S. delegate to the United Nations in 1958. "I understood better, I think, than others serving with me a great many things that motivated the hopes and pleas and demands of the little nations, particularly those whose people are dark-skinned." In 1963 she was awarded the Presidential

Appointed by President Dwight D. Eisenhower, Anderson served as a U.S. delegate to the United Nations in 1958.

Medal of Freedom by President Lyndon Baines Johnson, and in 1978 she received a Congressional Gold Medal for her "untiring and unselfish devotion to the promotion of the arts in this country during a distinguished and impressive career of more than half a century."

By then she had retired from the concert stage, following a farewell tour that began with a sold-out concert in Washington's Constitution Hall, where she had once been barred from singing. Asked if she had forgiven the DAR, Anderson replied, "Ages and ages ago. You lose a lot of time hating people."

From Washington her farewell tour went on to nearly fifty cities on four continents, ending on Easter Sunday, April 18, 1965, in New York's Carnegie Hall, where the cheering audience included two hundred family members and friends

A standing ovation at Anderson's farewell performance, Carnegie Hall, April 18, 1965.

seated in special boxes that Anderson had reserved for them. "When Miss Anderson sang the simple spiritual 'Hear de Lambs a-Cryin' in her deep, hollow, subterranean register . . . you felt it up and down the spinal column," wrote *New York Herald-Tribune* critic Alan Rich. "As always, she presented a stage picture of beauty, grace and generosity."

As a bonus following her Carnegie Hall retirement, Anderson performed that summer with her twenty eight year old nephew James DePreist, who had been asked to conduct the Philadelphia Orchestra at Robin Hood Dell, Philadelphia's outdoor amphitheater. Some years later, DePreist was engaged to conduct a series of concerts with Washington's National Symphony at Constitution Hall.

"I entered the stage door, conducted my rehearsal and returned to the hotel—three simple, normal acts denied to my aunt in 1939," DePreist recalled. "I called her to tell her how outraged, hurt, sorry, and grateful I was. 'It is inconceivable that you were not allowed to do what I've now so easily done,' I said. 'These concerts surely are as much yours as mine.' Her response was typical: 'Times have changed, and I am very, very happy for you.'"

After her retirement, while she no longer sang in public, Anderson remained in the public eye, speaking at colleges, music conservatories, and ceremonial events, and appearing for several years as narrator for Aaron Copland's musical tribute *A Lincoln Portrait*. She also made a point of helping young singers, particularly through the Marian Anderson Scholarship Fund, which she had started back in 1941 when the city of Philadelphia presented her with the $10,000 Bok Award, given annually to a Philadelphian who had performed "some service that redounds to the credit of the city."

In 1984, at the age of eighty-seven, Anderson accepted the first Eleanor Roosevelt Human Rights Award, given in memory of Mrs. Roosevelt in a ceremony at New York's City Hall. Before presenting the award, Mayor Edward I. Koch had to help Marian up from her wheelchair. "I have thanked my good Lord for [Mrs. Roosevelt] many times," she said. "I am only sorry the youngsters of today shall not have seen her in the flesh."

The roomful of guests at the ceremony applauded. Then everyone began to sing. They sang "He's Got the Whole World in His Hands," as Marian Anderson, standing at the podium, wept.

Orpheus Fisher, Marian's sweetheart and her husband of more than forty years, died in 1985 at the age of eighty-five. Marian stayed on at Marianna for

Marian Anderson received some fifty honorary degrees, beginning with her doctorate of music from Howard University in 1938. Here, at the age of ninety, she is awarded an honorary doctor of letters degree by the University of Connecticut, June 9, 1987.

several more years before moving to Portland, Oregon, to live with her nephew Jimmy, who had become music director of the Oregon Symphony.

She died on April 8, 1993, at the age of ninety-six, one day short of the 54th anniversary of the Easter concert at the Lincoln Memorial.

It had been said that her singing "seemed to come from the emotional center of each of us," and even after her death, her voice could not be stilled. At a memorial service in Carnegie Hall, attended by two thousand admirers, a silent piano stood at center stage, flanked by flowers. James DePreist told the crowd that on the single occasion when he and his aunt had discussed the idea of a memorial service, she had told him, "Jim, don't let them make a big fuss. And no speeches."

And so there were none. As DePreist left the stage, Marian Anderson's recorded voice rose up and filled the hall with the words of the spirituals she loved. Fourteen of her recordings were played with neither comment nor applause between them. And when the last one ended, the audience responded with a standing ovation.

Hand in hand, Marian Anderson and Franz Rupp
bow to an appreciative audience.

Eight
"WHAT I HAD WAS SINGING"

Marian Anderson never expected to become an activist in the struggle for equal rights. Away from the concert stage she valued her privacy and preferred a quiet family life. She disliked confrontations. And she never felt comfortable as the center of a public controversy.

"I would be fooling myself to think that I was meant to be a fearless fighter," she said in her autobiography. "I was not, just as I was not meant to be a soprano instead of a contralto."

Actually, Anderson had to fight hard to win her place in American music history. As she pursued her career, she was forced to challenge racial barriers simply to succeed as a singer.

When she was beginning her career in the 1920s, black artists in every field were excluded from the mainstream of American life. In films and on the vaudeville stage blacks were portrayed as comic dolts, stupid and lazy, unable to speak proper English, much less sing fluently in foreign languages. Like Roland Hayes, Marian Anderson stood in stately opposition to these insulting stereotypes, projecting an image of accomplishment and pride. Yet it was only after she toured Europe to great acclaim in the early 1930s that her artistry was recognized in her own homeland. And even then, Anderson's fame could not easily overcome the racial prejudice that she confronted as a black singer touring

America. Well into her career, she was turned away from restaurants and hotels.

Anderson's exceptional musical gifts and her uncompromising artistic standards made it possible for her to break through racial barriers. She became a role model, inspiring generations of African American performers who followed her. But it was the strength of her character, her undaunted spirit and unshakable dignity, that transformed her from a singer to an international symbol of progress in the advancement of human rights.

"Marian Anderson's superb professional triumphs were only a small part of what this great diva contributed to human understanding," said Leontyne Price, a black operatic superstar whose presence at the Met was taken for granted, thanks to Marian Anderson. "As a nation, we owe her gratitude for showing that talent and dignity can prevail and wrongs can be corrected."

Anderson's personal approach to her life and career was disarmingly modest and practical. "Certainly I have my feelings about conditions that affect my people," she told an interviewer. "But it is not right for me to try to mimic somebody who writes or who speaks. That is their forte. I think first of music and of being there where music is, and of music being where I am. What I had was singing, and if my career has been of some consequence, then that's my contribution."

He's got the whole world in His hands,
He's got the big round world in His hands,
He's got the wide world in His hands,
He's got the whole world in His hands.

He's got the wind and the rain in His hands,
He's got the sun and the moon right in His hands,
He's got the wind and the rain in His hands,
He's got the whole world in His hands.

He's got the gamblin' man in His hands,
He's got the lyin' man in His hands,
He's got the crap-shootin' man right in His hands,
He's got the whole world in His hands.

He's got the little bitsy baby in His hands,
He's got the little bitsy baby in His hands,
He's got the little bitsy baby in His hands,
He's got the whole world in His hands.

He's got you and me brother in His hands,
He's got you and me sister in His hands,
He's got you and me brother in His hands,
He's got the whole world in His hands.

He's got everybody in His hands,
He's got everybody in His hands,
He's got everybody here right in His hands,
He's got the whole world in His hands.

African American Spiritual

A kiss for Mom. Marian Anderson shows her mother the prestigious Philadelphia Medal, also known as the Bok Award, March 1941. The first African American to win the award, Marian used her prize money to establish a scholarship for young singers.

Chapter Notes

The following notes consist of citations to the sources of quoted material. Each citation includes the first and last words or phrases of the quotation, and its source. Unless otherwise noted, references are to works cited in the Selected Bibliography, beginning on page 101.

Abbreviations used are:

AH—*American Heritage* interview
Black—"Championing a Champion"
Keiler—*Marian Anderson: A Singer's Journey*
Lash—*Eleanor and Franklin*
LHJ—*Ladies' Home Journal* interview
MAP—Marian Anderson Papers at the University of Pennsylvania
ML—*My Lord, What a Morning*, Anderson's autobiography
Peggy Anderson—*The Daughters*
Roosevelt—*Eleanor Roosevelt's My Day*
Thernstrom—*America in Black and White*
Vehanen—*Marian Anderson: A Portrait*
White—*A Man Called White*

Chapter Two: Twenty-five Cents a Song

PAGE

5   "I did not hear . . . school": ML, p. 10

6   "Come and hear . . . ten years old": ML, p. 14

6   "I want her . . . seeing her": Keiler, p. 22

6   "I don't remember . . . all day long": LHJ, p. 77

6   "There were times . . . did not want us": ML, p. 39

7   "He was tall . . . our outings": AH, p. 51

9   "My sisters . . . would change": ML, p. 15

9   "She liked . . . Indian": ML, p. 16

11   "So I scrubbed . . . people": AH, p. 52

11   "Soon I was . . . expenditure": ML, p. 32

11–12 "This was . . . fourteen ninety-eight": ML, p. 30

12–13 "I knew . . . because I'm colored?": Anderson told about this incident a number of times and clearly still found the memory painful years later. This version is from LHJ, p. 173, and AH, p. 53.

14   "I sang . . . bird": ML, p. 24

15   "interested in . . . things like that": Keiler, p. 40

17   "I had heard . . . beyond repair": ML, p. 40

18   "[Marian] Anderson . . . Savannah": Keiler, p. 38

18   "I was busy . . . no great hurry": ML, p. 82

19   "I will make room . . . for anybody": ML, p. 49

Chapter Three: A Voice in a Thousand

PAGE

21   "These theater appearances . . . career": ML, p. 68

21–23 "On a daily basis . . . very quickly": the *Marian Anderson* video

24   "It is too much . . . long time": quoted in Keiler, p. 57

24–25 "I learned . . . indisposed": ML, p. 53

25   "[Miss Anderson] should . . . stage": Keiler, p. 6

25   "I was embarrassed . . . was over": ML, p. 74

25   "There came . . . back to singing": AH, p. 53

27   "with one part . . . upstairs": ML, p. 103

27   "Does 44A . . . song?": ML, p. 103

27   "We have won . . . finals!": ML, p. 104

27   "very smart . . . gaudy": ML, p. 105

27   "It was a thrill . . . fiasco": ML, p. 106

27–29   "A remarkable voice . . . last night": "Negro Contralto Shows Remarkable Voice at Stadium," *New York Herald-Tribune,* August 25, 1925

30   "It was an uncomfortable . . . my German": ML, p. 115

30–31   "One of the things . . . work anymore": AH, p. 55

31   "Mother and I . . . would help": ML, p. 112

Chapter Four: Marian Fever

PAGE

33   "There is no doubt . . . encores": MAP; Keiler, p. 81

34   "[My] high hopes . . . standstill": ML, p. 111

35   "I knew . . . found": ML, p. 131

36   "Accordingly . . . Baachsaal": ML, p. 137

36   "I did not know . . . marvelous": Keiler, p. 99

36   "Her command . . . sensation": Keiler, p. 99

36   "I have had . . . too much!": MAP; Keiler, p. 101

36   "One gets swept . . . little else": ML, p. 83

36   "From where . . . earth!": Vehanen, p. 22

37   "was a mixture . . . forget": ML, pp. 141 and 144

37   "The first visit . . . life": ML, p. 146

39   "My ceiling . . . voice": Vehanen, p. 28

39   "It was . . . leather": ML, p. 150

39   "If these people . . . better one": ML, p. 145

41   "The sight . . . he said": ML, p. 158

41   "A voice . . . hundred years": "Marian Anderson Is Dead at 96; Singer Shattered Social Barriers," *The New York Times,* April 9, 1993. According to Kosti Vehanen (p. 130), Toscanini said, "What I heard today one is privileged to hear only once in a hundred years," emphasizing the performance rather than the voice itself.

41   "I had gone . . . my own country": ML, p. 159

41   "a difficult . . . decision": ML, p. 160

41   "good and faithful friend": ML, p. 160

41   "You are making . . . will be?": Keiler, pp. 157 and 158

41   "Because I had . . . programs": ML, p. 16

42   "To tell . . . night": ML, p. 165

43   "Let it be said . . . honor her": "Marian Anderson in Concert Here," *The New York Times*, December 3l, 1935

43   "I studied . . . more careful": ML, p. 168

44   "Miss Anderson's . . . generation": Keiler, p. 180

45   "The look . . . describe": Vehanen, p. 220

45   "I shall never . . . she felt": Vehanen, p. 223–24

45   "My husband . . . finished artist": Roosevelt, p. 11

Chapter Five: Banned by the DAR

PAGE

51   "[Constitution Hall] stands . . . cultured people": Keiler, p. 192

53   "This is such . . . such a rule": Peggy Anderson, p. 113

       "Barring . . . is named": Keiler, p. 196

53   "As a foreigner . . . Anderson": MAP; Keiler, p. 195

53   "as contrary to . . . Columbia": Peggy Anderson, p. 116

53   "defend our . . . sing": MAP; Keiler, p. 201

54   "I regret . . . artist": Black, p. 724

54   "You had . . . failed": Black, p. 725

54   "I have been . . . resigning": Roosevelt, p. 113

55   "Of course . . . example": Peggy Anderson, p. 143

55   "I think . . . him up": Keiler, p. 207

57   "I don't care . . . sings": Black, p. 727

Chapter Six: Singing to the Nation

PAGE

59   "I was on my way . . . so far": ML, p. 185

59   "Music to me . . . beautiful": AH, p. 56

59   "I am not . . . world": MAP; Keiler, p. 203

60   "seemed to increase . . . went": ML, p. 187

60   "Do you feel . . . to do?": Vehanen, p. 278

60   "I did not . . . regret": ML, pp. 188–89

60   "I was sorry . . . gladly": ML, p. 187–88

60   "I said yes . . . had to appear": ML, p. 189

62   "My heart . . . to sing": ML, p. 190

62   "When I saw . . . the end": Vehanen, p. 242

62   "No member . . . exterior": White, p. 184

63   "Genius draws . . . today": "75,000 Acclaim Miss Anderson," *The Washington Post*, April 10, 1939. The concert, a local event, was featured prominently on the front page of *The Washington Post* but was accorded less importance by *The New York Times*, which carried the story on page 19 on the same day.

65   "She looked regal . . . than she was": Vehanen, p. 244

65   "There seemed . . . know how": ML, p. 19l

65   "My feelings . . . that she sang": the *Marian Anderson* video

68   "I have never . . . voice": quoted in Lash, p. 527

68   "I am so . . . again and again": "Throng Honors Marian Anderson in Concert at Lincoln Memorial," *The New York Times*, April 10, 1939

68–69 "As I did so . . . I can, too": White, p. 184

Chapter Seven: Breaking Barriers

PAGE

72   "for the highest . . . years": Keiler, p. 180

72   "It must be . . . difficulties": Black, p. 73l

74–75 "Last night . . . view": Roosevelt, p. 276

75   "The essential point . . . artist": ML, p. 193

75   "When I finally . . . sing in it": "Marian Anderson Is Dead at 96; Singer Shattered Racial Barriers," *The New York Times*, April 9, 1993

75   "We knew . . . married": ML, p. 83

75   "[Our marriage] was worth waiting for": ML, p. 83

75   "King and I . . . together": ML, p. 285

75   "When I see . . . daring": ML, p. 292

79   "I look . . . necessity": ML, pp. 239–40

80   "She didn't . . . around": Thernstrom, p. 62

80   "Somebody doesn't . . . feel it": AH, p. 53

80   "I was presented . . . join the group": LHJ, p. 174

80   "I believe . . . audience": Keiler, p. 257

82   "I was never . . . segregation": ML, p. 249

82   "It was . . . more to it": AH, p. 57

82   "Looking back . . . studying": ML, p. 306

85   "I understood . . . dark-skinned": LHJ, p. 176

86   "Ages and ages . . . people": "Marian Anderson' s Last Tour," *New York Herald-Tribune*, December 13, 1963

87   "When Miss Anderson . . . generosity": "Critic's View of Marian Anderson," *New York Herald-Tribune*, April 19, 1965

87   "I entered . . . happy for you": "Grounded in Faith, Free to Fly," *The New York Times*, April 18, 1953

87   "some service . . . city": Keiler, p. 229

87   "I have thanked . . . in the flesh": "Sentimental Ceremony for Marian Anderson," *The New York Times*, July 26, 1984

88   "seemed to come . . . of us": ML, from the 2002 edition Foreword by James Anderson DePreist, p. xv

88   "Jim, don't . . . speeches": "A Tribute to Marian Anderson, For the Most Part in Her Voice," *The New York Times*, June 8, 1993

Chapter Eight: "What I Had Was Singing"

PAGE

91   "I would be . . . contralto": ML, p. 188

92   "Marian Anderson's . . . can be corrected": "Professionally, Anderson Was the Mother of Us All," *The New York Times*, April 18, 1993

92   "Certainly I have . . . contribution": AH, p. 57

Selected Bibliography

Two books are essential reading for any student of Marian Anderson's life and career, and I am indebted to them both. Anderson's autobiography, *My Lord, What a Morning* (Urbana and Chicago: University of Illinois Press, 2002; originally published New York: Viking Press, 1956), ghost-written by music critic Howard Taubman, is based on extensive tape-recorded interviews that convey a powerful sense of Anderson's resolute spirit and dignity. The current edition has a foreword by Anderson's nephew, conductor James Anderson DePreist. This is an inspiring memoir for readers of all ages.

Allan Keiler's *Marian Anderson: A Singer's Journey* (New York: Scribner's, 2000), the only definitive biography, is the first truly complete, accurate, and documented account. Written with the cooperation of Anderson's family and with full access to her private papers, Keiler's book proved indispensable to my own research.

Other useful accounts include Kosti Vehanen's *Marian Anderson: A Portrait* (New York: McGraw-Hill, 1941; reprint Westport, Conn.: Greenwood Press, 1970), an affectionate memoir by Anderson's Finnish accompanist. Written soon after the Lincoln Memorial concert, Vehanen's book offers anecdotes and insights about Anderson's life on the international concert circuit. Walter White's *A Man Called White: The Autobiography of Walter White* (Athens, Ga.:

University of Georgia Press, 1995; originally published New York: Viking Press, 1948), by the civil rights activist who served as executive secretary of the NAACP, provides a vivid personal account of the events leading up to the Lincoln Memorial concert.

Two of Anderson's rare published interviews are particularly helpful in expressing her attitudes and experiences as a black performer in segregated America. "My Life in a White World," by Marian Anderson as told to Emily Kimbrough, appeared in the September 1960 issue of the *Ladies' Home Journal*. "A Voice One Hears Once in a Hundred Years: An Interview with Marian Anderson," by Barbara Klaw, appeared in the February 1977 issue of *American Heritage*.

Two informative scholarly articles are "Championing a Champion: Eleanor Roosevelt and the Marian Anderson Freedom Concert," by Allida M. Black, from the October 1990 issue of *Presidential Studies Quarterly*; and "A Marble House Divided: The Lincoln Memorial, the Civil Rights Movement, and the Politics of Memory, 1939–1963," by Scott A. Sandage, from the June 1993 issue of the *Journal of American History*.

Eleanor Roosevelt's syndicated newspaper columns are collected in *Eleanor Roosevelt's My Day*, edited by Rochelle Chadakoff (New York: Pharos Books, 1989). I also consulted Joseph Lash's *Eleanor and Franklin: The Story of Their Relationship* (New York: Norton, 1971). Harlow Robinson's *The Last Impresario: The Life, Times, and Legacy of Sol Hurok* (New York: Viking Press, 1994) offers many details and anecdotes about Anderson's relationship with her masterful American manager. And Peggy Anderson's *The Daughters: An Unconventional Look at America's Fan Club—the DAR* (New York: St. Martin's Press, 1974), provides an updated portrait of the women's organization that catapulted Marian Anderson into the political arena.

I found the following two books helpful in my discussion of race relations in the United States: *The Secret City: A History of Race Relations in the Nation's Capital,* by Constance McLaughlin Green (Princeton, N.J.: Princeton University Press, 1967); and *America in Black and White: One Nation, Indivisible,* by Stephan Thernstrom and Abigail Thernstrom (New York: Simon & Schuster, 1997).

Biographies for young readers of various ages include *Marian Anderson,* by Charles Patterson (New York: Franklin Watts, 1988); *Marian Anderson,* by Anne

Tedards (New York: Chelsea House, 1988); *Marian Anderson: Singer and Humanitarian,* by Andrea Broadwater (Berkeley Heights, N.J.: Enslow Publishers, 2000); *Marian Anderson: A Great Singer,* by Patricia and Fredrick McKissack (Berkeley Heights, N.J.: Enslow Publishers, 2001); and an exceptional picture-book biography, *When Marian Sang: The True Recital of Marian Anderson: The Voice of a Century,* by Pam Muñoz Ryan, pictures by Brian Selznick (New York: Scholastic Press, 2002).

Marian Anderson, a sixty-minute documentary video produced by WETA Washington, D.C., and broadcast by public television stations nationwide in 1991, features interviews with Anderson, Isaac Stern, Jessye Norman, and others, along with film clips of Anderson's performances on the concert stage and at the Lincoln Memorial. It is available from Kultur, 195 Highway 36, West Long Branch, N.J. 07764, phone (800) 573-3782, or from their website at www.kulturvideo.com.

The Marian Anderson Papers at the University of Pennsylvania in Philadelphia are the principal repository for documents concerning Anderson's career and personal life. The papers, filling 495 boxes, include personal and business correspondence, Anderson's journals, printed programs and posters, publicity material, newspaper clippings, scrapbooks, and memorabilia and are available to researchers at the university's Annenberg Rare Book and Manuscript Library. See www.library.upenn.edu/access/rbm.html.

Marian Anderson is the subject of several informative websites, which can be accessed by searching www.google.com for "Marian Anderson."

Selected Discography

SOME RECENT MARIAN ANDERSON RELEASES

This discography lists currently available CDs that are compilations of earlier recordings.

Marian Anderson: Schubert and Schumann Lieder, 1945–1951
(RCA #63575, 2000)
Includes a moving rendition of Schubert's "Ave Maria," one of Anderson's signature pieces, which she performed at the Lincoln Memorial concert and again at the White House in 1939.

Softly Awakes My Heart: Arias, Songs, & Spirituals, 1928–1946
(ASV Living Era #5262, 1999)
Includes arias ("O Don fatale") and spirituals ("Deep River," "Heav'n! Heav'n!") recorded in 1928, during Anderson's first trip to England.

Marian Anderson: Rare and Unpublished Recordings, 1936–1952
(Video Arts Intl #1168, 1999)
A variety of song types and languages, recorded when Anderson was at the peak of her vocal abilities.

Marian Anderson Spirituals, 1936–1952
(RCA #63306, 1999)
Includes studio recordings of the spirituals Anderson sang at the Lincoln Memorial: "De Gospel Train," "Trampin'," "My Soul's Been Anchored in the Lord," and her Lincoln Memorial encore, "Nobody Knows the Trouble I See."

The Lady from Philadelphia
(Pearl #9096, 1995)
Includes works by Purcell, Scarlatti, Bach, Handel, et al., along with traditional spirituals and familiar American songs such as "Carry Me Back to Old Virginny" and "My Old Kentucky Home."

Marian Anderson Spirituals: He's Got the Whole World in His Hands, 1961 & 1964
(RCA #61960, 1994)
Recorded in 1961 and 1965, shortly before Anderson's retirement.

Marian Anderson: Brahms Alto Rhapsody and Lieder/Sibelius Songs/Operatic Excerpts
(Pearl #9405, 1993)
Includes "O mio Fernando" from Donizetti's opera *La Favorita,* the aria that won Anderson the Lewisohn Stadium contest in 1925.

Marian Anderson: Bach, Brahms, Schubert, 1924–1955
(RCA #7911, 1990)
Includes one of Anderson's earliest recordings, "Go Down Moses" (1924), and her rendition of "Re dell' abisso affrettati" from Verdi's *Un Ballo in Maschera,* recorded with the Metropolitan Opera Orchestra on January 19, 1955, following Anderson's January 7 debut at the Met.

Acknowledgments and Picture Credits

My thanks to Nancy Shawcross and John Pollack of the Annenberg Rare Book & Manuscript Library at the University of Pennsylvania for their generous assistance in gathering research material and photographs for this book; to Antony Toussaint and the staff at the Schomburg Center for Research in Black Culture, a branch of the New York Public Library; and, as always, to the unfailingly helpful staff at the Prints and Photographs Division of the Library of Congress.

All photographs not specifically credited below were furnished by the Marian Anderson Collection, Annenberg Rare Book & Manuscript Library, University of Pennsylvania. All are hereby gratefully acknowledged.

The Schomburg Center for Research in Black Culture, New York Public Library: pp. 2, 17, 22, 66–67, 104

Prints and Photographs Division, the Library of Congress: pp. ii, 10, 13, 40, 48, 49, 52, 81

Index

Note: Page numbers in **bold** type refer to illustrations.

Academy of Music, Philadelphia, 24
Aeolian Hall, New York, 26, 27
African Americans:
   after slavery, 6
   and civil rights movement, 3, 71,
     80–82, 84–85, 91–92
   converts to Judaism, 10, **10**
   discrimination against, 3, 6, 12–13,
     14, 15, 17, 21, 23, 30, 47–48,
     51, 53–55, 59–60, 72, 75, 79–82,
     87, 91–92
   financial grants to, 35
   and Jim Crow laws, 15, 17, **17**, 21,
     22, 51, 80, **81**
   Marian as symbol for, 60, 69, 71,
     72, 87, 92
   stereotyped media portrayals of, 91
   vertical seating as compromise to,
     81–82

African American spirituals, 1, 14, 18,
   24, 40, 68, 85, 87, 89, 93
"America," 65, 68
Anderson, Alyse (sister), 6, **7**, 23, 30,
   43, 62
Anderson, Anna (mother), 7, **31**, **43**,
   94
   house for, 23–24
   and husband's death, 8–9
   jobs of, 11, 19, 30–31
   and Lincoln Memorial concert, **58**,
     62
   and Marian's childhood, 6, 9
   and Marian's finances, 11–12, 19,
     23, 30–31
   meeting the president, 45
Anderson, Benjamin (grandfather), 10
Anderson, Ethel May (sister), 6, **7**, 23,
   30, 62

Anderson, Harold (uncle), 7
Anderson, Isabella (grandmother), 9, **9**
Anderson, John (father), 6, 7–8, **8**
Anderson, Marian, ii, 7, **15, 16, 29,**
    31,32, 42, 43, 44, 56, 57, 74, 84,
    89, 90, 104, 108
  autobiography of, 91
  awards and honors to, 18, 35, **50,**
    70, 72, 85–86, 87, **88, 94**
  birth and early years of, **4,** 6–12
  and civil rights movement, 80–82,
    84–85, 91–92
  clothes for, 11–12, 27, 65
  concert programs, **20, 26, 28,** 36,
    46, 61, 68, 72
  concert tours of, 21, 23, 30, 36–41,
    39, 44, 59, 72, **73,** 77–81, **78,**
    79, 82, 84, 86–87
  Congressional Gold Medal to, 86
  critical reviews of performances by,
    18, 24, 25, 27, 29, 30, 36, 43,
    75, 87
  death of, 88
  European trips of, 30, 31, 33–41,
    34, 39, 46, 77, 91
  farewell tour of, 86–87, **86**
  financial assistance to, 11–12, 13,
    14, 19, 35–36
  as goodwill ambassador for State
    Department, 77–78, **78**
  house bought by, 23–24
  income of, 11, 19, 23, 30–31
  Lincoln Memorial concerts of, **x,** 1,
    2, 3, 56–57, **57,** 60, **61,** 62–69,
    63, 64, 66–67, 71
  and love of music, 5, 13, 15
  at Marianna Farm, 75, 77, 87

Anderson, Marian (*cont.*)
  marriage of, 75, **76,** 87
  memorial service for, 88–89
  Metropolitan Opera debut of, 82, 83
  Presidential Medal of Freedom to,
    85–86
  racial discrimination against, 12–13,
    17, 21, 23, 30, 51, 53–55, 59–60,
    75, 79–81, 87, 91–92
  radio performances by, 44, 71, 77
  recording contract of, 24
  retirement of, 86–87
  as role model, 92
  schooling of, 5, 6–7, 11, 14–15, 19,
    19
  and singing career, 12, 18, 21, 24,
    25, 30, 31, 34, 36, 41, 49, *75,*
    91, 92
  speaking engagements of, 87
  strength of character of, 92
  as symbol of her people, 60, 69, 71,
    72, 87, 92
  as United Nations delegate, 85, **85**
  vocal range of, 5, 27, 36, 43
  vocal technique of, 14, 18, 24–25,
    29, 37, 40–41, 43, 44, 92
  voice lessons for, 12, 13–14, 18–19,
    24–25
Anderson, Mary (aunt), 5–6, **9**
Armstrong High School, Washington,
  D.C., 51, 53
Arthur Judson Agency, 34
"Ave Maria" (Schubert), 68

Bach, Johann Sebastian, 36
Bachsaal, Berlin, 36
Baker, Josephine, 33

Bell Telephone Hour, The (radio), 77
Bethel Methodist Church, Danbury, Connecticut, 75
Bethune, Mary McLeod, 54, 80
Bing, Rudolph, **83**
blacks, *see* African Americans
Boghetti, Giuseppe, 18–19, 24–27, **24,** 30
Bok Award, 87, **94**
Budapest, Hungary, concert in, **39**
Burma, concert tour in, **78**

Canada, concert tours of, 82
Carnegie Hall, New York:
    concerts in, 43, 86–87, **86**
    memorial service in, 88–89
CBS television, 78
Central High School, Washington, D.C., 53, 55
Chapman, Oscar, 56, 62
Chicago Conservatory of Music, 18
Civil Rights March (1963), 84–85
civil rights movement, 3, 71, 80–82, 84–85, 91–92
Congressional Gold Medal, 86
Constitution Hall, Washington, D.C., **48, 74**
    Marian excluded from, 3, 45, 47–48, 51, 53, 55, 59–60, 72
    Marian's concerts in, 72, 74–75, 86
    National Symphony concerts at, 87
    "whites only" clause removed by, 82
Copland, Aaron, 87

Daughters of the American Revolution (DAR), **49**
    China Relief concert for, 72

Daughters of the American Revolution (*cont.*)
    and Constitution Hall, *see* Constitution Hall
    Marian's forgiveness of, 86
    Mrs. Roosevelt's resignation from, 54–55, **55,** 59, 71–72
    racial discrimination by, 3, 47–48, 51, 53, 54, 59–60, 72
"Deep River" (spiritual), 18
DePreist, James, 87, 88–89
Don Carlo (Verdi), 33
Duncan, Todd, 65

Eisenhower, Dwight D., 85
Eleanor Roosevelt Center, New York, **84**
Eleanor Roosevelt Human Rights Award, 87
Elizabeth, Queen of England, 72
Enwall, Helmer, 38, **38**
Enwall, Therese, 38
Europe:
    concerts in, 33, 36–41, 44, 45, **46,** 77, 91
    "Marian fever" in, 38
    study in, 30, 31, 33, 34–36

Far East, concert tour of, 78
Fisher, Orpheus "King," 18, 36, **37,** 75, **76, 78,** 87
Flagstad, Kirsten, 53
Ford Hour, The (radio), 44
Fort Logan Air Force Base concert, **73**
Foster, Stephen, 14

General Motors Hour, The (radio), 44

George VI, King of England, 72
Georgia State Industrial College, 15
German lieder, 14, 30, 35, 36
"Getting to Know You," 78
"Gospel Train" (spiritual), 68

Hackley, Emma Azalia, 6
Hayes, Ronald, **13**
   in Europe, 12, 33
   as mentor and role model, 12, 14,
      18, 40, 91
   singing career of, 12
"Hear de Lambs a-Cryin'" (spiritual),
      87
"He's Got the Whole World in His
      Hands" (spiritual), 85, 87, 93
Holy Land, visit to, 77
Howard University, Washington, D.C.:
   and Constitution Hall, 48–49, 51, 53
   honorary degree from, **50,** 88
   as sponsor of Marian's concerts,
      48–49, 51, 53, 54, 55, **61**
Hunter, Alberta, 33
Hurok, Sol, 41, 49, 55, **56,** 59, **74**

Ickes, Harold L., **52**
   and DAR, 53
   as Interior secretary, 51, 56
   and Lincoln Memorial concerts, 3,
      56–57, 63, **63,** 68, 84
   memorial service for, 84
"I Have a Dream" speech (King), 85
India, concert tour of, 77
Interior Department, U.S., 56, 60
Israel, concerts in, 77

Japan, concerts in, 77

Jim Crow laws, 15, 17, **17,** 21, **22,** 51,
      80, **81**
Jofe, Isaac A., **74, 78, 79,** 80
Johnen, Kurt, 35, **35**
Johnson, Lyndon B., 86
Johnston, V. D., 51
Julius Rosenwald Fund, 35

King, Martin Luther, Jr., 85
King, William L. "Billy," **23**
   as Marian's accompanist, **20,** 21, **28,**
      30, 41
   and racial discrimination, 21, 23,
      30, 41
   on the road, 21, 23, 30, 34
Koch, Edward I., 87

La Favorita (Donizetti), 26
Lewisohn Stadium, New York, 25, 27,
      28, 29, 68
Lincoln, Abraham, 3, 85
Lincoln Memorial, **58**
   and equal rights, 51, 71
   Ickes memorial service at, 84
   Marian's concerts at, **x,** 1, **2,** 3,
      56–57, **57,** 60, **61,** 62–69, **63, 64,**
      66–67, 71, 84–85
Lincoln Portrait, A (Copland), 87

Marian Anderson Citizens' Committee,
      53
Marian Anderson Scholarship Fund, 87
Marianna Farm, Danbury,
      Connecticut, 75, **76,** 87
Marie Jose, Crown Princess (Italy), 40
Masked Ball, A (*Un Ballo in
      Maschera*) (Verdi), 82, **83**

Metropolitan Opera, New York, 82, **83**, 92

"My Day" (E. Roosevelt), 45, 54, 71–72, 74–75

"My Soul Is Anchored in the Lord" (spiritual), 68

National Association for the Advancement of Colored People (NAACP):
awards to Marian from, **70**, 72
in struggle against racial discrimination, 51, 53, 54

National Music League, contest of, 25–27, 68

National Park Service, 1, 60

National Symphony, Washington, D.C., 87

NBC radio network, 77

Negroes, *see* African Americans

New York Herald-Tribune, 29, 87

New York Philharmonic Orchestra, 25, 28

New York Times, The, 43

"Nobody Knows the Trouble I See" (spiritual), 68

Norfolk Journal and Guide, 71

O'Day, Caroline, 62

"O mio Fernando" (Donizetti), 26, 27, 68

Oregon Symphony Orchestra, 88

Paris Opera, **46**

Parks, Rev. Wesley, 11

Patterson, Mary Saunders, 13–14

Payne, John, 33, **34**

People's Chorus, Philadelphia, 6, 11, 14

Perkins, Francis D., 29

Philadelphia Medal (Bok Award), 87, **94**

Philadelphia Orchestra, 87

Philharmonic Society, 24

Pinchot, Gifford, 62

Pittsburgh Courier, 55

Pons, Lily, 33

Presidential Medal of Freedom, 85–86

Price, Leontyne, 92

Quirinal Palace, Rome, 40

Reifsnyder, Agnes, 14

Revolutionary War, U.S., 47, 54

Rich, Alan, 87

Robert, Mrs. Henry M., Jr., 53, 54

Robin Hood Dell, Pennsylvania, 87

Robinson, Alexander, 5

Robinson, Jackie, 82

Roosevelt, Eleanor, **52**, **70**, 84
awards in memory of, 87
death of, 84
influence of, 54–55, 71–72
and Marian's concerts, 3, 44, 45, 51, 53–54, 57, 63, 72, 74–75
"My Day" column by, 45, 54, 71–72, 74–75
racial discrimination opposed by, 51, 54
resignation from DAR, 54–55, **55**, 59, 71–72
and royal visitors, 72
speaking tours of, 82, 84

Roosevelt, Franklin D., 3, 45, 57

Rubinstein, Arthur, 33
Rule Rasmussen, 36
Rupp, Franz, 72, **73**, **74**, **78**, **79**, 80,
    90, 108

Salzburg Festival, Austria, 40
Savannah Morning News, 18
Schubert, Franz, 14, 68
Schumann, Elisabeth, 33
Sibelius, Jean, 39
slavery, end of, 6
"Solitude" (Sibelius), 39
South America, concerts in, 44, 77
South Philadelphia High School for
    Girls, 14–15, 19, **19**
Spingarn Medal (NAACP), **70**, 72
Stanton Elementary School,
    Philadelphia, 5, 11
State Department, U.S., goodwill tour
    for, 77–78, **78**
Stern, Isaac, 23

Taubman, Howard, 43
Toscanini, Arturo, 40–41, **40**
Town Hall, New York, 25, **26**, 27, 29,
    41–43
"Trampin'" (spiritual), 68

Un Ballo in Maschera (*A Masked Ball*)
    (Verdi), 82, **83**
Union Baptist Church, Philadelphia:
    contributions to Marian's career by,
        11, 12, 19
    Marian's membership in, 5, 6, 7, 11
    soloists in, 12

United China Relief Fund, 72, 74
United Nations, 85, **85**
University of Connecticut, honorary
    doctorate from, **88**

Vehanen, Kosti:
    at Lincoln Memorial, **x**, **2**, 62, 65,
        66–67
    as Marian's accompanist, **x**, **2**, 38,
        39, 41, **42**, 62, **66–67**
    as music scout, 36–37
    retirement of, 72
    traveling, 41, **42**
    at White House, 45
Verdi, Giuseppi, 14, 82
Victor Talking Machine Company, 24

Wanamaker's Department Store,
    Philadelphia, 11, 30
Washington, D.C.:
    Civil Rights March (1963) in, 84–85
    "I Have a Dream" speech in, 85
    Marian's concerts in, **x**, 1, **2**, 3,
        56–57, **57**, 60, **61**, 62–69, **63, 64,
        66–67**, 71, 72, 74–75, 84–85, 86
    racial discrimination in, 17, 47–48,
        51, 53–55
Washington Times-Herald, 51
West Indies, concerts in, 77
White, Walter, 51, **52**, 53, 54, 55, 56,
    62, 68–69
William Penn High School,
    Philadelphia, 14
Wilson, Lucy Langdon, 18
World War II, concerts during, 72, **73**

The Negro Community Chorus

of Duquesne

PRESENTS

Marian Anderson

CONTRALTO

William L. King at the Piano

Carnegie Music Hall
Duquesne, Pa.
Saturday Evening, April 23, 1921
at eight fifteen

RUSSELL FREEDMAN was aware that Marian Anderson was one of the great vocal artists of the 20th century. He hadn't thought of writing a book about her, however, until he found out about the encounter between her and Eleanor Roosevelt that led to the Lincoln Memorial concert and established Anderson as a seminal figure in the civil rights movement.

Mr. Freedman is the acclaimed author of more than 40 nonfiction books for young people, including *Lincoln: A Photobiography*, a Newbery Medal Book, and two Newbery Honor Books, *The Wright Brothers: How They Invented the Airplane* and *Eleanor Roosevelt: A Life of Discovery*. He is also the recipient of the Laura Ingalls Wilder Award for his body of work. Mr. Freedman lives in New York City.